Beyond Words

Teacher's Book

Certificate reading and listening skills

Alan Maley and Alan Duff

Cambridge University Press

Cambridge

London   New York   New Rochelle

Melbourne   Sydney

Published by the Press Syndicate of the University of Cambridge
The Pitt Building, Trumpington Street, Cambridge CB2 1RP
32 East 57th Street, New York, NY 10022, USA
296 Beaconsfield Parade, Middle Park, Melbourne 3206, Australia

© Cambridge University Press 1976

First published 1976
Fourth printing 1983

First printed in Great Britain by
Fakenham Press Limited, Fakenham, Norfolk

Reprinted in Great Britain at the
University Press, Cambridge

ISBN 0 521 20986 2 Teacher's Book
ISBN 0 521 20985 4 Student's Book
ISBN 0 521 20988 9 Cassette 1
ISBN 0 521 21249 9 Cassette 2

Copyright

Acknowledgements

Extracts are reproduced by permission of the following:

p. 3, Mr David Attenborough and *The Listener*; p. 7, Times Newspapers Ltd; p. 11,
Times Newspapers Ltd; p. 15, *TV Times* and Mr Peter Laurie; p. 20, Times
Newspapers Ltd; pp. 23, 31, 58, Dr Lyall Watson and Hodder & Stoughton Ltd; p. 26,
Peter Shaffer. Copyright © Peter Shaffer Ltd 1964, Hamish Hamilton, London; p. 35,
E. A. Ritter, *Shaka Zulu* (Longman, 1955), pp. 66–8. Copyright © The Estate of E. A.
Ritter, 1955. Reprinted by permission of Penguin Books Ltd and Garlicke &
Housfield; p. 46, William Collins Sons & Co. Ltd; p. 50, reprinted by permission of
Faber & Faber Ltd; p. 63, Weidenfeld & Nicolson Ltd; p. 71, James Britton, *Language
and Learning* (Pelican, 1972), pp. 36–9. Copyright © James Britton, 1970. Reprinted
by permission of Penguin Books Ltd; p. 77, permission of Mr Carlo Bavagnoli; pp. 82,
86, from C. F. Stoneman, *Space Biology* (Biology Topic Books, 1972), pp. 72, 38.
Copyright © C. F. Stoneman, 1972. Reprinted by permission of Penguin Books Ltd.

Contents

Preface

Beyond Words is intended to prepare students to understand written and spoken English at upper intermediate level.

We start from the notion that there are generalisable features of both the written and spoken modes. A familiarity with these features allows the student to apply his knowledge as a strategy for dealing with any text. Hence, although the comprehension questions specific to any given text are important, we regard as even more important the exercises which develop overall strategies of listening and reading. These exercises include work on word formation, linguistic cohesion in texts, and the thematic structure of texts.

Control of vocabulary has been exercised by reference to the *Cambridge English Lexicon*. Any word not included in this list, but retained in passages for contextual reasons, is given special attention through an exercise or a question. All passages have been adapted to meet these requirements.

The book covers a wider area than the bare requirements of an examination, such as the Cambridge First Certificate, reading and listening comprehension papers. It will certainly be useful as a preparation for such examinations, but we hope that it will also be used by upper intermediate students without this specific examination interest.

In the past too much attention has been paid to the details of comprehension both in spoken and written language. Inevitably, this has led to concentration on words and specific structural devices within sentences. But it is clear that the ability to understand is closely related to the ability to see overall patterns of meaning, and to relate bits of meaning forward and backward in a text. We hope that the two books of *Beyond Words* go some way towards preparing students to exercise these major pathfinding strategies and to developing in them a healthy disrespect for words as such.

A.M.
A.D.

Introduction

Beyond Words consists of two books, one for the teacher and one for the student. There is also a recording (available on cassette or open reel) of the listening comprehension texts contained in the Teacher's Book.

Student's Book

All the Reading comprehension units come at the beginning of the book, and all the Listening comprehension units at the end. However, the corresponding units of Reading and Listening are intended to be used together.

Each Reading passage is linked thematically with a Listening text. In this way, the student first meets the information in its written form and is in some way prepared for meeting some of it again, in a modified version, in the spoken form. For example, 'Battery buses' is a written text; 'Atomic cars' the parallel spoken text. Both deal with a common theme – the alternatives to petrol-driven vehicles. Both contain a certain amount of common vocabulary and even syntax. We hope that this juxtapositioning of spoken and written texts will ease the task of the student, and perhaps also inculcate the habit of comparing and contrasting what he sees and hears in general in the foreign language.

Each unit is organised as follows:

Text
Multiple choice
True or false?
Vocabulary in context
Summary

Listening comprehension units are found in a separate section of the book and are organised as follows:

Multiple choice
True or false?
Vocabulary in context
Summary or discussion

Clearly, the 'Multiple choice' questions are the sections most closely connected with the Cambridge examinations. 'True or false' questions are however also necessary since there are many points of comprehension which it is impracticable to test by the multiple choice procedure. The 'Vocabulary in context' section is important since it is an attempt to train the student to retrieve meanings from context, and to wean him away from the idea that a word or phrase has some sort of pre-ordained and immutable meaning.

Teacher's Book

In this book the internal organisation is different. Here each Reading unit is accompanied by its corresponding Listening unit.

The format is as follows:

Unit 1: Reading comprehension
Detectives' lives – fact and fantasy
Answers to Reading comprehension questions
Open-ended questions
Language building
Summary and discussion

Unit 1: Listening comprehension
The reality of being a detective
Answers to Listening comprehension questions
Language building
Expansion exercise
Discussion

We attach particular importance to the 'Language building' sections, which are intended to develop the generalisable strategies referred to above.

The 'Expansion exercises' are an attempt to teach active listening by encouraging the student to reconstitute the full text from fragmentary portions.

How to use the books

The following are minimal suggestions for exploiting the materials. For a teacher with few class hours, however, they are probably sufficient. In other cases the teacher will obviously wish to elaborate upon them and devise procedures to suit his own particular circumstances.

Reading comprehension

Before asking students to look at the text, write the title on the blackboard and ask them to guess what it is likely to be about. In this way anticipations about what is to be read will already have been set up, and the reading task motivated.

For each text let students read at their own pace. Suggest however that they skim the passage first to see roughly what it is about, and then read it carefully for its full meaning. Only then go on to the 'Multiple choice' questions. When these are finished, the 'True or false' questions should be tackled *orally*, without referring to the text. Often the points being dealt with in this section are the same as the ones in the 'Multiple choice' questions. This is intentional. The 'True or false' questions are exercises as well as tests. They have a pedagogical function of re-activating what has just been read. If the answer is *false*, the student should say *why* it is false. After the two sections of questions, give the answers. Students should mark their own or each other's work.

'Vocabulary in context' and 'Language building' must clearly be done by close reference to the text, as must the 'Summary'. The 'Summary' is best done in the student's own time, not in class, in order to save time.

At the end compare the anticipations which the students had based on the title with the actual text. How accurate were their predictions?

Listening comprehension

Read the text aloud, or play the unpaused version of the recording, *twice*. This is as it will be for the Cambridge examination. Then pass immediately to the 'Multiple choice' questions.

Then play the unpaused recording once again. Students then do the 'True or false' questions with the teacher orally.

The 'Language building' sections will normally need constant reference to the text. To assist the teacher in this a version of the text has been recorded *with pauses*. This version should also be used for the 'Expansion exercises'. In detail the procedure would be:

Play the first sentence of the text.

Read the shortened version of it from the Teacher's Book and invite students to lengthen it to its original form. This will usually be done in stages with students recalling different blocks, and only gradually focussing in on the original. For example, in Unit 1 the first sentence is:

'I met an Englishman in the mountains of central New Guinea who had been away from European company for about six years.'

After hearing this once, and being read the prompt: 'I met an Englishman', the students might be expected to expand like this:

Student 1   I met an Englishman in Guinea.
  Teacher   Guinea?
Student 2   I met an Englishman in *New* Guinea.
  Teacher   Good. Yes?
Student 3   I met an Englishman in the mountains of New Guinea.
  Teacher   Good. Anyone else?
Student 4   I met an Englishman in the mountains of New Guinea who had been away . . .
  Teacher   Yes?
Student 5   . . . for six years.
  Teacher   Good. I'll repeat it now. Try to remember the rest . . . etc.

Once you are satisfied with the version you are given, replay the original sentence on the tape and pass to the next one. This reactivation of syntactic patterns has a very useful backwash effect on the student's oral ability. It is also a useful way of drawing attention to the basic or kernel sentences underlying the more complex realisations.

Of course, if time does not permit, there is no need to do the whole of the 'Expansion exercise'. But even a little is beneficial.

(Note that although the shortened sentences given in the Teacher's Book usually follow the Listening passage sentence for sentence, it may happen that a few sentences are omitted or combined with others by conjunctions.)

Unit 1: Reading comprehension

Answers to 'Tall tales from the backwoods'

Multiple choice: 1c; 2c; 3c; 4a; 5b

True or false? 1. false; 2. false; 3. true; 4. false; 5. false; 6. true; 7. true; 8. false; 9. false; 10. false

Vocabulary in context: 1c; 2a; 3b; 4a; 5d; 6a

Open-ended questions

1. Why did Roger always ask his friends the meaning of obscure and difficult words?
2. Why did Taz spend a night with the Oxford Dictionary?
3. Was Taz surprised when Roger woke him up?
4. What is the meaning of the title of this passage?

Language building

1. The language of this passage is informal and intimate. Words are used loosely, as in speech, because the author is telling a story. Many turns of phrase are characteristic more of spoken than written English. Draw students' attention to the following:

. . . *one of these* (ghost towns) (line 3). 'One of these/those' usually indicates *familiarity* with the object in question, e.g. 'one of those little shops where they sell everything', 'one of those things for taking out spots'.

. . . *that's about all, except* . . . (line 5). This is the equivalent of saying: 'there is no more to be said about that' or 'there is no need to know anything else'.

. . . *this friend of mine* (lines 7, 8). The only difference between 'this friend of mine' and 'my friend' is that the former is more casual, more intimate; 'my friend' would seem stiff and formal here. Other such expressions often heard are: 'this mate of mine'; 'this brother of his'; 'this business of theirs'.

actually . . . (line 12). This word is the colloquial equivalent of 'in fact', but is often used simply as a hesitation marker, e.g. 'I don't know, actually, but I think . . .' 'Actually, I'd rather not, if you don't mind . . .' It can also be used instead of 'well' in many cases.

just . . . (line 12). This use of 'just' meaning 'barely', is very common in speech. The opposite is 'not quite', usually in the form of 'didn't quite'. Get students to make sentences using 'didn't quite' and 'just' on the basis of the information given below.

I

1. Pass mark = 50		Election results	
A	 49	A	.... 143 votes
B	 76	B	.... 142 votes
C	 51	C	.... 9 votes

2. Phrasal verbs are most effectively used in this passage. Draw attention to the following:

laid out (line 4). Does 'laid out' mean the same as 'constructed'?

turned up (lines 4, 11). What is the difference between 'turned up' and 'arrived'?

wandering about (lines 8, 9). Does 'about' add anything to the meaning of wandering?

settled down (line 11). What is the effect of 'down'?

push off (line 13). Is there any difference between 'push off' and 'leave'?

went by (line 21). Could the word 'passed' have been used here?

fed up with (line 24). Would the meaning be changed if 'tired' or 'sick of' were used?

got in the way of (line 14). This, clearly, means the same as 'interfered with'. What difference, if any, is there between these words?

3. *Upturned*
This word is derived from 'turn' + 'up', without any change of meaning in spite of the reversed word order. Other common examples of this kind of construction are:

overblown	uplifted
downtrodden	downcast (see line 20, 'cast down')
overthrown	overcast
inbuilt	overlaid

4. *Outback*
Students should have no difficulty in deducing the meaning of 'outback' from the context as there is a logical connection between this word and 'in the middle of the Australian desert'. Words such as this are easily formed in English, e.g.

indoors	overhead
upstairs	underground

5. *No-hoper* (line 8)
Words of this kind are easily coined in English, usually by the addition of the suffix '-er' to a compound of verb + some other part of speech, e.g.

do-gooder	all-rounder
go-getter	non-starter
back-slider	pacemaker

6. *D'you happen to know?* (line 19)
'D'you happen to . . .' often prefixes a question when the speaker half expects a negative answer. It occurs frequently with verbs such as 'have', 'know', 'see', e.g. 'D'you happen to have last week's *Times*?' 'D'you happen to have seen a small grey cat round here?'

7. Notice the special use of 'would' for repeated actions in the past:
'. . . half-a-dozen guests a year *who would ride up* on horseback . . .'
'. . . if there was a pause in the conversation *he would look at you*'
'Roger *would ask* him . . . and he *would have to admit* . . . and Roger *would be very pleased*'.

8. *Glinting* (line 34)
If students are not sure of the meaning of this word, ask them what they understand by 'a steely grasp'. What is Roger feeling at this moment? (For further practice in descriptive words of this kind see the Language building notes to the Unit 18, Reading comprehension passage, 'Sunrise on the Veld'.)

Unit 1: Listening comprehension

Three sacks of carrots

I met an Englishman in the mountains of central New Guinea who had been away from European company for about six years. He had established a very good working relationship with the local people, who were Pygmies. He had had three or four visitors during those six years. We came, with a line of porters, down the mountainside: the porters sing as they march, so that he knew we were coming for hours before we actually arrived. He was extremely excited. He was a little fat man with curly grey hair. He bounced up and down with excitement and, perhaps because he hadn't spoken English to anybody else for a long time, his words stumbled out across one another, so that he never finished a sentence. He stuttered: 'S-so g-glad, c-come, s-sit.'
   He was most friendly and he took us into his hut, which was filthy dirty, and sat us down. Then he said: 'W-would you chaps like a drink?' and he produced some bottles of red wine – claret. It was an extraordinary thing to produce in remotest New Guinea. Whisky you can understand . . .
   'S-stupid blokes on the c-coast', he said. 'I had one of these medical chaps to see me – he comes through once every year or so – and he looked at my eyes and said: "What you want, Jim, is–is–is carrots. They'll help you to–to see better." Now, you can't grow carrots up here so I got on the radio to the store on the coast and I said: "S–send me three sacks of c-carrots." But the stupid fool thought: "What's Jim asking for carrots for? He must mean claret." So they dropped sixty bottles of claret from an air drop.'
   We tucked into his claret and helped him over that particular problem. 'Glad you could get rid of some of it,' he said. 'I can't stand the stuff.' Then, next morning, we set off again, with our porters. As we were going, I looked back and there was Jim, outlined against his hut, waving rather sadly . . .
(From an article by David Attenborough in *The Listener*)

Answers to 'Three sacks of carrots'

Multiple choice: 1c; 2c; 3a; 4d

True or false? 1. false; 2. true; 3. true; 4. true; 5. false; 6. true; 7. false; 8. true; 9. false; 10. true; 11. false; 12. true

Vocabulary in context: 1c; 2d; 3a; 4b; 5b

Open-ended questions

1. Why did Jim stutter?
2. The sentence: 'Whisky you can understand . . .' is left unfinished. Ask the students to suggest what the speaker had in mind.
3. Why did Jim have to radio to the coast for carrots?
4. Why did the wine have to be dropped from an aeroplane?
5. Why did Jim look sad when his guests left?

Language building

1. Notice the recurrence of certain features mentioned in the notes to the Reading comprehension passage 'Tall tales from the backwoods'.

one of these medical chaps. The listener is expected to know what kind of person the speaker has in mind.

actually ('He knew we were coming . . . before we actually arrived'). Here 'actually' simply strengthens the meaning of 'before' and indicates some surprise on the part of the speaker.

2. *Filthy dirty*
Strictly speaking, this is unnecessary repetition, i.e. filthy = very dirty. Such expressions, however, are occasionally met in everyday speech, e.g. tiny little; great big.

3. *(I) can't stand the stuff*
This is a stronger way of saying: 'I don't like it'. Get students to practise 'I can't stand . . .' in this emphatic form. Make use of some of the following suggestions if you like: unpunctuality; untidiness; inquisitiveness; greediness.

Remember to teach different ways of saying the same thing, e.g. on unpunctuality: 'I can't stand people who come late.' 'I can't stand it when you come late.' 'I can't stand being kept waiting.'

4. *Stuttered*
(See the list of similar onomatopaeic words in the notes to the Unit 17 Reading comprehension passage 'Our first words'.) Draw attention to the connection between 'stuttered' and 'his words stumbled out across one another'.

5. *He bounced up and down . . .*
What nouns are normally associated with the verb 'bounce'? How is it possible for a man to bounce? What movements would he be making?

Expansion exercise

1. I met an Englishman . . .
2. He had a relationship.
3. He had three or four visitors.
4. We came down the mountainside.
5. He knew we were coming.
6. He was excited.
7. A little man.
8. He bounced . . .
9. Because he hadn't spoken English for a long time . . .
10. He stuttered . . .
11. He took us into his hut.

12. And he produced some bottles of red wine.
13. It was an extraordinary thing.
14. I had one of these chaps to see me.
15. What you want is carrots.
16. You can't grow carrots.
17. I got on the radio.
18. The stupid fool thought . . .
19. They dropped sixty bottles.
20. We helped him.
21. I can't stand . . .
22. We set off.
23. As we were going, I looked back . . .

Unit 2: Reading comprehension

Answers to 'The underworld'

Multiple choice: 1b; 2c; 3c; 4a

True or false? 1. false; 2. false; 3. true; 4. false; 5. true; 6. false; 7. true

Vocabulary in context: 1a; 2c; 3b; 4c; 5c; 6a; 7b; 8c; 9c

Open-ended questions

1. Why is the Earth's outer layer of rock thought to be 'as thin as the skin of an apple'?
2. How is it possible to conclude from the way in which earthquake waves travel that the centre of the Earth is probably not solid?
3. What happens on the surface of the water when a stone is dropped into a pond?
4. How is it possible to reduce the number of casualties in earthquakes?
5. What causes the intense heat at the centre of the earth?

Language building

1. *Flattened* (line 3)
Verbs derived from adjectives often take the suffix '-en'. Students should be encouraged to bring such verbs into their active vocabulary. The following words are all useful examples:

deaden	broaden
quicken	lengthen
sharpen	deepen

2. *Tremors* (line 27)
This word should automatically come up in the preliminary discussion of the subject 'Earthquakes'. Remind students that the less common word 'quake' is in fact a synonym for 'tremor'.

3. The following verbs all express a particular kind of movement:

hurtle (line 1)	descend (line 16)
spin (line 2)	clamber (line 33)
radiate (line 14)	penetrate (line 37)
pulsate (line 16)	

Examine each word carefully in context, then try to define the movement in your own words. Ask yourself:
Is the movement regular or irregular, smooth or uneven?
Is it repetitive? fast or slow?
Does it involve energy, effort, patience?

What other things/persons can move in the same way?

4. Notice the use of 'were' in the following sentences:

Thus if you *were* to stand at sea level at the North or South pole you *would be* 13 miles nearer the centre of the Earth than if you stood on the Equator. (line 3)

So great is the heat at 10,000 feet that *were* it not for an elaborate air-conditioning system, the miners there *would be* roasted. (line 39)

This use of the subjunctive in English is more common in the written language. Try to reword these sentences to suit the spoken language.

Discussion

1. In what parts of the world do earthquakes still occur?
2. What are volcanoes?
3. What measures can be taken to prevent the great damage caused by earthquakes?
4. What is meant by the phrase 'natural disasters'?

Unit 2: Listening comprehension

Darwin ruined by Cyclone Tracy

As preparations began yesterday for evacuating 25,000 people from the north Australian city of Darwin, devastated by a 165 m.p.h. cyclone on Christmas Day, it became clear that the death and destruction was due almost as much to human factors as to the violence of the wind.

People in Darwin had become so accustomed to cyclone warnings that few of them paid attention to the radio warnings of Cyclone Tracy's approach, which began early on Christmas Eve. Many people, in fact, died in their cars as they tried to drive home through the cyclone from Christmas parties or social calls.

Since Townsville was devastated by a cyclone in December 1971, sparking off a public outcry in Australia for an adequate warning system, the meteorological authorities have regularly issued alarms of every dangerous cyclone. But because few of the cyclones ever hit the coastal towns, people there had come to ignore the warnings.

Darwin's last alert was broadcast only two weeks before Cyclone Tracy – and on that occasion the storm changed direction and headed off harmlessly down the coast. According to one man, local inhabitants were actually joking about the alert on Christmas Eve and even making up songs to the effect that cyclones never got to Darwin.

Apart from those people killed in their cars, nearly all the other victims died in the wreck of their homes which, despite the fact that Darwin lies in the recognised cyclone belt, had not been built to withstand cyclonic winds. Although building standards in other states of Australia were made much stricter after the tragedy at Townsville, the Darwin authorities never followed the new regulations. Consequently, most of suburban Darwin was built of light wood and corrugated iron raised off the ground on piles to give coolness in the tropical climate. And the sides of the houses were simply nailed to the roof instead of being firmly attached with what Australian builders call 'cyclone bolts'. As a result, many people were killed by flying sheets of iron from the roofs.

(From an article in *The Sunday Times*)

Answers to 'Darwin ruined by Cyclone Tracy'

Multiple choice: 1b; 2d; 3b; 4c
True or false? 1. false; 2. false; 3. false; 4. true; 5. false; 6. true; 7. true

Vocabulary in context: 1b; 2b; 3a; 4c; 5b; 6c

Language building

1. *Idioms and expressions*
Draw students' attention to the following expressions:
a) 'People in Darwin *had become* so *accustomed* to cyclone warnings . . .'
b) 'People there *had come to ignore* the warnings . . .'
c) 'Local inhabitants were . . . even making up songs to the effect that cyclones *never got to* Darwin.'

Notice how each of the phrases in italics refers to a cumulative experience.
a) This is a straightforward example. Several words in the language are used in a similar way, e.g. used, reconciled, bored, devoted.
b) This phrase is more idiomatic. 'Had come to ignore . . .' means 'had gradually developed the habit'.
Remind students of similar expressions, e.g. 'I gradually came to like him.' 'After a while I came to see what they were trying to do.' 'In the end, they came to accept him as the new director.'
c) This, too, is idiomatic. Here the cumulative experience is of something which does *not* take place. The past simple of many verbs may be used in this way.

2. Notice how much information is conveyed through the adjectival use of nouns:

north Australian city	cyclone belt
cyclone warnings/radio warnings	building standards
165 m.p.h. cyclone	Darwin authorities
warning system	Australian builders

Such combinations are particularly common with figures, place names, and measurements, e.g.

a New York lawyer	a 10-foot wall
a £5000 contract	a Devonshire farmer

3. Notice the use of the following words, which are almost synonymous in this context: alert; alarm; warning.

Practise the verbs commonly associated with these words, e.g.: to sound; to give; to raise; to issue.

4. *Human factors*
The word 'factor' is often used to replace 'element' or 'reason'. Remind students of phrases such as: the time factor; the speed factor; the health factor.

Expansion exercise

1. As preparations began . . . it became clear.
2. People had become accustomed to warnings.
3. Few of them paid attention.
4. Many people died.
5. Since Townsville was devastated . . . the authorities have issued alarms.
6. . . . few cyclones hit the coastal towns.
7. Darwin's last alert was broadcast . . .
8. The storm changed direction.
9. Local inhabitants were joking.
10. All victims died in their homes.
11. . . . which had not been built to withstand winds.
12. Although building standards were made stricter . . .
13. Suburban Darwin was built of wood.
14. The sides of the houses were simply nailed to the roof.
15. Many people were killed.

Discussion

Refer back to the Reading comprehension text. In the light of what you have learnt from both passages, discuss the question of 'natural disasters'. Consider, in particular, the improvements that could be made in the construction of houses and buildings in regions where earthquakes and cyclones frequently occur.

Unit 3: Reading comprehension

Answers to 'When you have an accident'

Multiple choice: 1b; 2b; 3b; 4c; 5c

True or false: 1. false; 2. false; 3. false; 4. false; 5. false; 6. false; 7. false

Vocabulary in context: 1a; 2b; 3a; 4c; 5b; 6d; 7b

Open-ended questions

1. What are some of the most common causes of accidents?
2. What is the connection between road construction and traffic accidents?
3. In what circumstances are you obliged to stop after an accident?
4. What is the excuse given by drivers that the courts are reluctant to accept?
5. Why is it advisable to wait for the police to arrive after an accident?

Language building

1. Draw attention to the following idiomatic expressions:
a) *to the point* (line 3) = apt or pertinent
   Remind students of other idioms, such as: stick to the point; off the point; get to the point.
b) *plays its part* (line 9) = has an effect.
c) *come out* (line 16) = become revealed, show up.
'Come out' often suggests emergence from a state of hiding or concealment. This is why it is associated with nouns such as: truth, answer, facts, etc.

2. Notice the use of 'self' in:
somebody other than *yourself* . . . (line 20)
the driver *himself* . . . (line 24)
and you *yourself* . . . (line 34)

3. Consider the following lines from the passage:
a) There are, firstly, *the legal formalities of exchanging names and addresses* . . . and . . . informing the police (lines 17, 18)
b) . . . if a driver continues *unaware of causing injury* . . . (line 23)
c) . . . you must give your name . . . to anyone who has *a good reason for requesting it* (line 28)
d) The police are *expert at drawing plans, taking measurements* . . . (line 32)

Ask students to reword the sentences from which these examples are taken. Wherever possible, they should avoid using the constructions in italics.

Remind students of other words used with the preposition 'at' in much the same way as 'expert at': good at, clever at, quick at, handy at, etc.

Discussion

1. What other common causes of accidents can you think of in addition to those mentioned in the passage?
2. What can be done to make roads safer?
3. Are there any traffic regulations you consider unnecessary or even harmful?

Unit 3: Listening comprehension

Speeding

Less than eighty years ago a man called Walter Bersey was taken to court in London for driving at a speed greater than 2 m.p.h. in the city and also, strangely enough, for not having a man with a red flag to walk in front of his car. Bersey was the last man to be summoned under the old Locomotives Act, which restricted speeds to 2 m.p.h. in towns and 4 m.p.h. in the country, and made it an offence to drive without a man with a red flag in front.

Parliament now increased the speed limit to 14 m.p.h. But by 1903 the development of the car industry had made it necessary to raise the limit to 20 m.p.h. By 1930, however, the law was so widely ignored that speeding restrictions were done away with altogether. For five years motorists were free to drive at whatever speeds they liked. Then in 1935 the Road Traffic Act imposed a 30 m.p.h. speed limit in built-up areas, along with the introduction of driving tests and pedestrian crossings.

Speeding is now the most common motoring offence in Britain. Offences for speeding fall into three classes: exceeding the limit on a restricted road, exceeding on any road the limit for the vehicle you are driving, and exceeding the 70 m.p.h. limit on any road. A restricted road is one where the street lamps are 200 yards apart, or less. One motorist measured the distance between two lamps and found that they were $201\frac{1}{2}$ yards apart. Unhappily for him he was told: 'The law does not concern itself with trifles.'

The main controversy surrounding speeding laws is the extent of their safety value. The Ministry of Transport maintains that speed limits reduce accidents. It claims that when the 30 m.p.h. limit was introduced in 1935 there was a fall of 15 per cent in fatal accidents. Likewise, when the 40 m.p.h. speed limit was imposed on a number of roads in London in the late fifties, there was a 28 per cent reduction in serious accidents. There were also fewer casualties and deaths in the year after the 70 m.p.h. motorway limit was imposed in 1966.

In America, however, it is thought that the reduced accident figures are due rather to the increase in traffic density. This is why it has even been suggested that the present speed limits should be abolished completely, or that a guide should be given to inexperienced drivers and the speed limits made advisory, as is done in parts of the USA. (From an article in *The Sunday Times* Magazine)

Answers to 'Speeding'

Multiple choice: 1a; 2d; 3b; 4d; 5c

True or false? 1. false; 2. false; 3. true; 4. true; 5. false; 6. false; 7. true

Vocabulary in context: 1b; 2a; 3c; 4b; 5c; 6a

Language building

1. This passage contains several useful pairs of verbs, many of which are antonyms.
Draw students' attention to:
raise or increase/reduce
abolish/impose
introduce/do away with

Point out, also, other useful examples of rewording, such as:

and $\begin{cases} \text{Parliament} \ldots \textit{increased the speed limit} \\ \ldots \text{the development of the car industry had made it necessary} \\ \textit{to raise the limit} \end{cases}$

and $\begin{cases} \ldots \text{speeding restrictions were } \textit{done away with altogether} \\ \text{motorists were } \textit{free to drive at whatever speeds they liked} \end{cases}$

and $\begin{cases} \text{speed limits } \textit{reduce} \text{ accidents} \ldots \\ \text{there was } \textit{a fall of 15\%} \text{ in fatal accidents} \ldots \\ \text{there was } \textit{a 28\% reduction} \text{ in serious accidents} \ldots \end{cases}$

Draw attention to the following nouns which are associated with the verbs above:
speed limit, speed(s), restriction(s), accidents, traffic density.

2. *Built-up*
This kind of adjective, formed from verb (participle) + preposition, is perhaps less
common in English than that which is formed from the same elements in the reverse
order, e.g. 'inbuilt'.
Remind students of the more common compounds of this type, such as:

grown-up	turned-up (nose, collar, etc.)
broken-down (car)	made-up (story)
broken-off	cut-out

(See also the language notes to the Unit 1 Reading comprehension passage 'Tall tales
from the backwoods'.)

Expansion exercise

1. A man was taken to court.
2. Bersey was the last man to be summoned . . .
3. The old Locomotive Act restricted speeds.
4. The law was ignored.
5. Motorists were free to drive.
6. The Road Traffic Act imposed a speed limit.

7. Speeding is the most common offence.
8. Offences for speeding fall into three classes . . .
9. A restricted road . . .
10. One motorist measured the distance.
11. He was told . . .
12. The main controversy is . . .
13. The Ministry of Transport maintains . . .
14. It claims . . .
15. When the speed limit was imposed in London . . .
16. There were fewer deaths.
17. Reduced accident figures are due to increase in traffic density.
18. Speed limits should be abolished.
19. A guide should be given.

Discussion

1. Is there any need for speed restrictions in big cities?
2. Is driving too fast any more dangerous than driving too slowly?
3. What methods are used by the police to catch drivers who break the speed limit?

Unit 4: Reading comprehension

Answers to 'Detectives' lives – fact and fantasy'

Multiple choice: 1c; 2c; 3b; 4c; 5c

True or false? 1. true; 2. false; 3. true; 4. true; 5. false; 6. false; 7. false; 8. true; 9. false; 10. true

Vocabulary in context: 1c; 2c; 3b; 4b; 5b; 6b

Open-ended questions

1. What are the three main differences between the life of the real detective and that of the 'cop' in TV plays?
2. Why is it necessary for a detective to have a sound training in law?
3. Why is it that in real life the police are less concerned with finding the criminal than they are on television?
4. Why are detectives overworked?
5. What does the author mean by 'unpleasant moral twilight'?
6. Why does society prefer to let criminals off with lighter sentences?

Language building

The style of this passage is informal, almost colloquial. Draw attention to:
1. *Idiomatic expressions and colloquialisms*

cops	spent in chatting . . .
scantily-clad	the story is over
stamp(ing) out crime	at all hours of the day and night
in real life	stay(ed) behind bars

2. *The use of 'have to'*
In more formal writing this use of 'have to' (expressing habitual action with an overtone of obligation) would not occur so frequently. Notice the following:
He has to know exactly what actions . . .
He has to know nearly as much law . . .
. . . *he has to apply it* on his feet . . .
He has to prove his case . . .
. . . *he often has to gather* a lot of different evidence . . .
. . . a detective *has to be out* at all hours . . .
. . . they always *have to behave* with absolute legality . . .
. . . most of them *have to break* the rules . . .

If the detective *has to deceive* the world . . .
. . . they *have to get* results . . .

This construction has clearly been heavily used (perhaps even overworked!) in the passage. Remind students of alternative ways of expressing obligation, and get them to use these alternatives in rephrasing the above sentences. The following may serve as a reminder:
to be obliged to
to be forced to
to be made to
to be expected to
to be required to
to have no choice but to . . .
need to
must

Discussion

1. What aspects of the TV detective's life bear least resemblance to those of the real detective's life, as shown in this passage?
2. What are some of the inconveniences of a detective's job?
3. What are the differences between the duties of a policeman on the beat and those of a detective?

Unit 4: Listening comprehension

The reality of being a detective

Another great difference between cops and their television counterparts is their physical condition. Detectives everywhere work twelve hours a day, seven days, most weeks. A study of British detectives' working hours found that they spent five hours a day at home. This means that detectives' marriages are often shaky affairs, and they are said to have the highest divorce rate of any professional group. And most real-life detectives, far from being the tanned, fit heroes of the screen, are white-faced and drawn, short of several weeks' sleep, and living on their nerves.

A detective's work is decided by the type of crime to which he is assigned. An officer working in a big city, either in Britain or America, will deal all day, every day, with assaults, robberies, thefts, murders – whatever comes his way. If he is assigned to a specialist unit, like the Murder Squad in London, his interests are centred on the people who commit those crimes, and the rest of the world passes him by.

The work he does is determined by the laws relating to those crimes, making it hard to compare the work in different countries. The training of detectives, too, is often quite different. When a British detective enters the force he will already have done his sixteen weeks' basic training. After two trial years on the beat he can join the CID – the Criminal Investigation Department – again on trial, and after two years, if he's good enough, become a detective constable. Then he has a further three months at a detective training school where the studies are almost entirely in criminal law, and the pass mark is 80 per cent. As a diversion, the students get occasional lectures on murder investigations and the use of explosives, but the rest is hard grind.

However, in New York there is much less formal training. A young policeman gets a few weeks in school, mainly learning self-defence and the basic powers of arrest. He then starts learning his trade in earnest on the streets. If he is 'active' there, he can be tried out in the detective department – there is no school. If he learns fast, he stays. As you'd expect, the American earns more than his British counterpart. It's difficult to compare exactly: a hard-working detective sergeant in London can earn, counting overtime, up to £4500 a year. In New York, the same man would get about £7200. But many do not have to rely entirely on their salaries, as recent events in American cities have shown. In Chicago, forty-eight policemen have been convicted in the past three years, and 407 fired or forced to resign. For them, police wages are just pocket money: their real income comes from the underworld.
(From an article by Peter Laurie in the *TV Times*)

Answers to 'The reality of being a detective'

Multiple choice: 1c; 2c; 3b; 4c; 5c

True or false? 1. true; 2. false; 3. true; 4. false; 5. false; 6. false; 7. true; 8. false; 9. true

Vocabulary in context: 1a; 2b; 3c; 4c; 5a; 6c; 7a; 8b; 9c

Language building

1. . . . and they *are said to have* the highest divorce-rate . . .
Phrases such as this, expressing qualified opinion, are often heard on news broadcasts.
Here are some other examples:
known to be/have
believed to be/have
understood to be/have
considered to be/have
thought to be/have
reputed to be/have
assumed to be/have
(See also language notes to the Unit 20 Reading comprehension passage, 'The dangers of space', and the Unit 7 Listening comprehension passage, 'Pizarro and the Inca gold'.)

2. The following sentence in paragraph 1 may give difficulty: 'And most real-life detectives, far from being the tanned, fit heroes of the screen, are white-faced and drawn, short of several weeks' sleep, and living on their nerves.'

Play it over several times, then ask students:
a) to state briefly the main point of the sentence
b) to *deduce* the correct meaning of:
far from being
tanned
white-faced and *drawn*
short of several weeks' sleep

Make use of the following suggestions if you like:
far from being
not wishing to be
quite unlike

much better than
unable to imitate

tanned
exhausted by sleeplessness
browned by the sun
powerfully built
well-known

drawn
aesthetic looking
hollow-cheeked
red-eyed
ugly

short of several weeks' sleep
lacking several weeks' sleep
unable to sleep for several weeks
able to go without sleep for several weeks
refreshed after several weeks' sleep

c) to consider further uses of 'far from + -ing' and 'short of', e.g.:
far from being satisfied, he demanded even more money . . .
far from apologising, they tried to throw the blame on us . . .
Point out that this is a somewhat formal way of saying: *not only . . . but . . .*

Draw attention to the nouns most commonly associated with *short of* (meaning *wanting* or *lacking*):
short of *money/funds*
short of *time*
short of *petrol*
short of *members/support*
short of *plates/knives/glasses* etc . . .

3. Notice the use of *tense* in this passage. The present tense is frequently used for the same purpose as the passive in more formal language, e.g.
Then he *has* a further three months . . . = then he *is trained* for a further three months.
A young policeman *gets* a few weeks . . . = a young policeman *is given* a few weeks . . .
As a diversion, the students *get* occasional lectures = as a diversion, the students *are given* occasional lectures.

Notice, particularly, the conditional construction with 'if' + present tense. Students are often wrongly tempted to use the future in such cases:
If he is assigned to a specialist unit . . .
and . . . *if he's good enough*, become a detective constable.
If he is active there, he can be tried out . . .
If he learns fast, he stays.

4. *Divorce-rate*
This type of compound, using *-rate* as a suffix, often occurs in semi-technical writing. (See also the language notes to Unit 16 Reading comprehension passage, 'Population growth and industry'.)

Expansion exercise

1. Another difference is . . .
2. Detectives work most weeks.
3. A study found . . .
4. Detectives' marriages are shaky affairs.
5. Most detectives are living on their nerves.
6. A detective's work is decided by . . .
7. An officer will deal with whatever comes his way.
8. If he is assigned to a specialist unit . . .
9. The work he does . . .
10. The training is quite different.
11. When a detective enters the force . . .
12. After two years he can become a detective constable.
13. He has three months.
14. Students get lectures.
15. In New York . . .
16. A policeman gets a few weeks . . . mainly learning . . .
17. If he is active . . .
18. If he learns fast . . .
19. The American earns more.
20. It's difficult to compare . . .
21. Many have to rely on their salaries.
22. In Chicago policemen have been convicted.
23. Police wages are pocket money.

Discussion

1. Get students to refer back to the Reading comprehension passage and make a second list of statements about the life of a policeman or detective. From these two lists, construct a short 'portrait' of a detective.
2. Detective films never cease to be popular. What makes a good detective film?

Unit 5: Reading comprehension

Answers to 'Oil wealth flows up the Voe'

Multiple choice: 1c; 2b; 3b; 4c; 5b

True or false? 1. false; 2. true; 3. false; 4. false; 5. true; 6. true

Vocabulary in context: 1c; 2b; 3b; 4b; 5c; 6c; 7: 'as far away from London as Corsica'; 8b; 9d; 10b

Language building

Consider the following:
newly signed	oil fired
gift bearing	high powered
better paid	newly opened
oil related	long awaited

Get students to explain in their own words the meaning of these compound adjectives. Suggest other similar compounds (noun + participle, adjective + participle, adverb + participle), e.g. power-driven, highly qualified, newly married, short-lived.

Open-ended questions

1. What does 'this particular labour shortage' refer to?
2. 'A giant oil complex' – which paragraph describes this complex in detail?
3. 'This archipelago' refers to
a) Sullom Voe
b) Corsica
c) Shetland

Discussion

Using the information gained from both the Reading and the Listening comprehension passages, discuss the problem of exploiting oil. Consider, also, the various industries that are partly or wholly dependent on oil.

Unit 5: Listening comprehension

The curse of the islands

Contrary to what many people believe, Shetland is far from being an economically depressed area. And oil is not an unrelieved blessing: it has brought its problems.

The traditional fishing industry has recently been enjoying a great boom, and the Shetlanders have begun setting up their own processing factories. This means that most of the profits now stay on the islands instead of going to the Aberdeen fish merchants. Processing factories could not have been so profitable without a sudden demand for fish from new, mostly foreign markets. Large quantities of cod are sold to Western Europe to be made into fish fingers. But the biggest market of all is for haddock in the United States. This delicious, firm-fleshed fish is apparently all the rage in American sea-food restaurants, while fish and chips, so Shetlanders claim, has overtaken the hamburger as the favourite national snack.

Fishing on Shetland is a two-and-a-half million pound a year industry. Almost all fishermen work on a sharing basis and earn considerable profits from their hard and dangerous work. Their wives work in processing factories or in the knitwear industry, which is also enjoying a boom. Even this year, when the oilmen are present more as single spies than in battalions, their operations have clashed with those of the fishermen. There is only very limited space for ships at the piers, and increasingly the oil supply ships are occupying it. If a fishing boat cannot unload quickly and put to sea again, money is lost.

The main fear of the Shetlanders, however, is that workers will abandon local industry during the first few years of the oil boom, wrecking the fish processing factories and the knitwear business. It would be difficult, maybe impossible, to revive those industries when the oil boom was over. And if the oilmen start to try tempting the crews of fishing boats with higher pay, then there may be trouble.

Shetlanders are worried by the threat that oil represents for the environment. No oil company has yet revealed the likely consequences of its actions. Beaches, and the sea itself, are in fact likely to be polluted with oil from spillings from tankers at sea and from the ship-to-shore pipelines at places like Sullom Voe. It is worth reflecting that the recent prosperity of Shetland's fishing industry is due in part to the destruction of Massachusetts' own fishing industry by oil and industrial pollution.

Finally, a few words on oil and the 'national interest'. The Shetlanders prospered during the Second World War because Britain needed their fish and knitwear. Both are basic industries meeting human needs far more important than the supply of petrol, jet fuel, plastics, or central heating. Both industries are creative. They require imagination, and, in the case of fishing, courage. These qualities, so typical of the Shetlands, would seem to be more in the national interest than holding down the price of a gallon of petrol, or keeping up the production of plastic cups and the provision of fuel for Concorde aircraft.

(From an article in *The Sunday Times* Magazine)

Answers to 'The curse of the islands'

True or false? 1. false; 2. true; 3. false; 4. false; 5. false; 6. false; 7. false; 8. false; 9. true; 10. true; 11. false

Multiple choice: 1d; 2c; 3b; 4b; 5a

Language building

1. Get students to explain the meaning of the following, preferably by suggesting synonyms:

boom   clash
on a sharing basis   wreck
all the rage   prosperity

Suggest words and expressions which mean the opposite of the above.

2. Ask students to suggest interpretations for the phrase in italics in the sentence below.
'Even this year, when oilmen are present more *as single spies than in battalions*, their operations have clashed with those of the fishermen.'
If necessary, consult a Dictionary of Quotations to discover the origin of this expression.

3. 'The *crews* of fishing boats . . .'
'Crew' is a group noun, usually applied to the men who work on a ship (or plane or spacecraft). Draw attention to other group nouns, such as: staff, team, gang, group etc.

Expansion exercise

1. Shetland is not a depressed area.
2. There has been a boom in fish.
3. The profits stay on the islands.
4. Processing factories are profitable.
5. Fishermen work on a sharing basis.
6. Their wives work in factories.
7. The oil men are present.
8. There is mooring space.
9. Labour will abandon local industry.
10. The oil men try tempting the crews.
11. Shetlanders are alarmed.
12. Beaches are likely to be polluted.
13. The prosperity of Shetland's fishing industry is due to the destruction of Massachusetts's industry.
14. The Shetlanders prospered.
15. Both are basic industries.
16. They require imagination.
17. These qualities are in the national interest.

Discussion

1. What differences in attitude do you notice between the Reading comprehension text and this one?
2. Do you agree with the conclusions reached by the author of the Listening text? Why?

Unit 6: Reading comprehension

Answers to 'Eyeless sight'

Multiple choice: 1c; 2c; 3c; 4c

True or false? 1. false; 2. false; 3. false; 4. false; 5. false; 6. false; 7. true; 8. true; 9. false; 10. true

Vocabulary in context: 1c; 3: 'distinguish'; 4: 'blindfolded'; 5: Jim Peters; 7b

Open-ended questions

1. Why is the phenomenon 'obviously not new'?
2. What was it that started Rosa on her path to fame?
3. Why was the final demonstration the most convincing?

Language building

1. *'Differentiate between coloured lights'*
There are two synonymous phrases in the first paragraph. Ask students to identify them. (Tell the difference between . . ./ distinguish different colours.)
2. Ask students to name a 'celebrity' in each of the following fields: cinema, theatre, sport, literature.

3. *A medical board*
The word 'board' can be applied to a number of other groups of people:

a selection board	a board of selectors
an examining board	a board of examiners
an interviewing board	a board of governors
a governing board	a board of discipline
a disciplinary board	a board of inquiry

In all of these there are a number of underlying layers of meaning involved:
a *board* is a group
contains the idea of consultation
contains the idea of power over those who come before it

Another word similar in meaning is 'panel', e.g.: a panel of doctors, a panel of judges or celebrities (on TV or radio).

4. Ask the students to work out the meaning of 'winced' from the context by careful questioning, e.g.:
Is wincing the result of something pleasant or unpleasant?
Does your facial expression change when you wince?

What do you do when someone shines a bright light in your eyes?

Does the exclamation 'ouch!' go with wincing?

Do the same with 'screen', again using clues provided by the context. (There are two types of screen here, one general, one specific.)

5. Draw attention to the suffix '-ist': neuro*list*, psycho*logist*.

It is common for specia*lists* to form the name of their specialty in this way, e.g.: chemist, geologist, biologist, zoologist, etc.

Note, however, *physician* = a doctor

whereas *physicist* = a scientist concerned with physics.

Discussion

Expand on the discussion topic of the Unit 12 Listening comprehension passage 'Telepathy'.

Unit 6: Listening comprehension

Colour and feelings

The fact that blind people can 'see' things using other parts of their bodies apart from their eyes may help us to understand our feelings about colour. If they can sense colour differences then perhaps we, too, are affected by colour unconsciously.

Manufacturers have discovered by trial and error that sugar sells badly in green wrappings, that blue foods are considered unpalatable, and that cosmetics should never be packaged in brown. These discoveries have grown into a whole discipline of colour psychology that now finds application in everything from fashion to interior decoration. Some of our preferences are clearly psychological. Dark blue is the colour of the night sky and therefore associated with passivity and calm, while yellow is a day colour with associations of energy and incentive. For primitive man, activity during the day meant hunting and attacking, which he soon saw as red, the colour of blood and rage and the heat that came with effort. So it was natural that green, the complementary colour to red, should be associated with passive defence and self-preservation. Experiments have shown that colours, partly because of their physiological associations, also have a direct psychological effect. People exposed to bright red show an increase in respiration rate, heartbeat, and blood pressure; red is exciting. Similar exposure to pure blue has exactly the opposite effect; it is a calming colour. Because of its exciting connotations, red was chosen as the signal for danger, but closer analysis shows that a vivid yellow can produce a more basic state of alertness and alarm, so fire engines and ambulances in some advanced communities are now rushing around in bright yellow colours that stop the traffic dead.

(From *Supernature*, by Lyall Watson)

Answers to 'Colour and feelings'

Multiple choice: 1a; 2b; 3c; 4d

True or false? 1. true; 2. true; 3. false; 4. false; 5. false; 6. true; 7. false; 8. true; 9. false

Vocabulary in context: 1c; 2c; 3d; 4c

Language building

1. 'Bright' has the synonym 'vivid' in the passage, and 'exciting' has the antonym 'calming'. Give students the word 'bright' and see if they can identify the synonym. If not, tell them. Do likewise with 'exciting'.

2. 'Because of its exciting connotations . . .'
Which word from the passage means the same as 'connotations'?

3. Draw attention to the alternative ways of expressing the same thing:
. . . associations of (energy, etc.) . . . associated with (passivity, etc.)
. . . people exposed to . . .   . . . exposure to . . .

4. Draw attention to the compound 'self-preservation'.
'Self' enters readily into compound words, e.g. self-destructive, self-willed, self-taught, self-denying, self-satisfied. It is therefore worth looking out for. (See also language notes to Unit 11 Listening comprehension passage 'How lions live'.)

5. Note: psychology (noun) – psychological (adj.)
         physiology (noun) – physiological (adj.)
Many nouns in '-ology' form adjectives in the same way, e.g.: geology, ecology, biology, sociology.

Expansion exercise

1. Blind people can 'see' things using other parts of their bodies.
2. Perhaps we too are affected.
3. Manufacturers have discovered that sugar sells badly.
4. These discoveries have grown into a discipline.
5. Some preferences are psychological.
6. Dark blue is associated with passivity.
7. Yellow is a day colour.
8. Activity during the day meant hunting.
9. It was natural that green should be associated with defence.
10. Colours have a psychological effect.
11. People show an increase.
12. Exposure to blue has the opposite effect.
13. Red was chosen as the signal for danger.
14. Fire engines and ambulances are rushing around in yellow.

Unit 7: Reading comprehension

Answers to 'Gold'

Multiple choice: 1c; 2b; 3c; 4a; 5b; 6c

True or false? 1. false; 2. true; 3. false; 4. true; 5. false; 6. false; 7. true; 8. false; 9. true; 10. false

Vocabulary in context: 1a; 2b; 3b; 4a; 5c; 6d; 7b; 8d; 9a

Open-ended questions

1. Why have men always longed to store gold at home?
2. Why is gold so expensive to produce?
3. What are the main observable characteristics of gold?
4. The gold standard was not immediately adopted after Sir Isaac Newton established a fixed price for the metal. Why was this?
5. Why do Italian jewellers burn their wooden floors?
6. Why did Bernard Shaw advise the gentlemen 'to vote for gold'?

Language building

1. '*Often the only rule in young California . . .*'
The meaning of this sentence may not be immediately evident to students. Lead them towards the meaning by asking questions such as:
1. What was the gold rush?
2. What kind of people took part in the gold rush?
3. What does *young* California mean?
4. Is a *mob* the same as a crowd? What difference is there between the two words?
5. What is the connection between *rope* and the exercise of *rule*?

2. *Supertanker*
'Super-' as a prefix is freely used in everyday speech. It literally means 'above' but usually has the meaning of 'extra large' or 'exceptional'. Ask students to suggest compounds with 'super-'. The following suggestions may be useful:

supermarket	supersonic
superstructure	superannuation
supertax	

3. *Reportedly*
Remind students of similar adverbs, such as:

allegedly	apparently
presumably	reputedly

4. The word 'translucent' is an economical substitute for the longer phrase 'so thin that light passes through it' (line 10).

The prefix 'trans-' usually has the meaning of through, across, or over. Consider the following words: in what context would you find them, and what would they mean?

transparent	transcribe
transverse	transmit
transformation	transfuse
transcontinental	transplant

Notice, also, the use of 'ex-' in combinations such as 'ex-prisoner', 'ex-guard'. This prefix is common to both written and spoken language, particularly before words such as:

president	headquarters
(world) champion	capital
pilot	leader
Parisian	guard

5. Idioms

In many languages the word 'gold' appears in a number of idioms or idiomatic expressions. Some of the most common in English are:

(the) golden handshake
a heart of gold/as good as gold
a golden chance/opportunity
silence is golden
a golden wedding anniversary
all that glitters is not gold

Discussion

1. What qualities does gold *not* have?
Compare gold to other metals, e.g. silver, mercury, lead, from the point of view of: physical properties/qualities; usefulness; availability.
2. Is the gold standard likely to change? If so, what could replace it? Would any nations in particular benefit or suffer from such a change?

Unit 7: Listening comprehension

Pizarro and the Inca gold

It is probable that Francisco Pizarro was born in 1471. What is certain is that he was illegitimate and that he grew up in very poor surroundings. He was first heard of as a soldier in 1510. A year later he was a member of the exploration party which discovered the Pacific. It may have been at this point that Pizarro first heard of the existence of Peru, for tradition suggests that some captive Indians spoke of a great kingdom to the south. But the rulers in Spain were more interested in discovering a passage through to the Pacific, and the story of Inca gold was discounted as another of the vague rumours that started in New Spain.

These stories, however, were not lost on Pizarro. In 1524 he left Panama and sailed south into unexplored waters. This first voyage was extremely difficult but, despite the heavy seas, Pizarro beat his way farther south along the Pacific coast than anyone before him. They did obtain some crude gold ornaments from the few natives they captured but, more important, Pizarro received confirmation of the existence of a great empire farther south, an empire rich beyond imagining with gold.

Upon his return to Panama, plans were immediately agreed upon to gain the approval and support of the royal court of Charles V of Spain. Pizarro made his trip back to Spain in 1528 and, though King Charles never fully grasped the significance of his report, permission was hesitantly granted for a third voyage. The King refused to provide Pizarro with any financial assistance. In all history there can be no more marked example of such a mean investment bringing such a golden reward.

When Pizarro landed in 1531 at Tumbez he was immediately encouraged by the news of a fierce civil war within the Inca empire. With the death of the Inca chief – the Sapa Inca – two brothers had fought for the leadership. The civil war, which had been a terribly bloody affair, had ended with a fierce battle in the northern Andes. For this reason the chief of the Incas was no longer a thousand miles to the south of Tumbez, but only three hundred and fifty miles away in the mountains. Pizarro could not have been more fortunate; the state was still very disturbed and the Sapa Inca lay just within reach.

Systematically the Spaniards set out to strip the nation of its wealth. Temples were stripped of their treasures, towns were plundered and burnt, and famine and disease broke out among the natives. Inevitably the thieves disagreed and split into two opposing camps, those supporting Pizarro and those standing behind his former colleague Almagro. In the end, both leaders suffered sudden and violent deaths during the course of their struggle.

There remains one final irony to the Pizarro story: the gold which had flooded Spain with such an abundance of wealth was responsible for her eventual ruin. With this surfeit of gold, prices rose, inflation began, and Spain started on a steady economic decline from which she took a long time to recover.
(From the introduction to *Royal Hunt of the Sun*)

Answers to 'Pizarro and the Inca gold'

Multiple choice: 1b; 2d; 3a; 4c; 5b

True or false? 1. true; 2. true; 3. false; 4. true; 5. false; 6. true; 7. false; 8. false

Vocabulary in context: 1b; 2b; 3d; 4a; 5b; 6b; 7b; 8c

Language building

1. *Style*
Notice, particularly in the opening paragraph, the cautious and circumspect style characteristic of speculative writing. The following phrases should be pointed out to students:

it is probable that . . .
what is certain is that . . .
it may have been . . . that . . .
. . . tradition suggests that . . .

(See also Unit 20 Reading comprehension, 'The dangers of space', Language building, no. 8)

2. *Permission . . . granted*
Students should be encouraged to learn to associate words that frequently occur together. Thus, for example, 'permission' is associated with the verbs:

grant	refuse
give	request/ask for
get	

What verbs are commonly associated with the following nouns?
advice
information
help

3. *No more marked example*
'Marked' here has the meaning of 'striking' or 'outstanding'. Other words associated with 'marked' are:
a marked man (a wanted man)
a marked improvement (definite)
a marked success (considerable)
a marked increase (evident)

4. *Plundered*
The exact meaning of this word should become clear through answering the question: 'What was the main aim of Pizarro's expedition?'

5. *Abundance*
This word is not one which the students are likely to need in their active vocabulary. Its meaning, however, can be easily deduced from 'flooded' in the same sentence and 'surfeit' in the following sentence.

Expansion exercise

1. Francisco Pizarro was born
2. He was illegitimate
3. He was a soldier
4. A year later
5. At this point Pizarro first heard
6. Tradition suggests
7. But the rulers in Spain
8. The story was discounted
9. These stories, however
10. This voyage was difficult but
11. They did obtain some gold ornaments
12. But, more important
13. Plans were immediately agreed upon
14. Pizarro made his trip back . . . and . . . permission was granted.
15. The King refused
16. There can be no more mean example
17. When Pizarro landed he was encouraged
18. The two brothers had fought
19. The civil war had ended
20. The chief of the Incas was only three hundred and fifty miles away
21. The state was still disturbed
22. The Spaniards set out
23. Temples were stripped
24. The thieves disagreed
25. Both leaders suffered sudden deaths
26. There remains one irony
27. The gold . . . was responsible
28. Spain started on an economic decline . . .

Discussion

Both the Reading and the Listening comprehension passages mention the bad effects of the sudden discovery of gold. Do you know of any other examples of nations which have suffered in a similar way through the discovery of a metal or raw material in great abundance?

Unit 8: Reading comprehension

Answers to 'Flicker'

Multiple choice: 1c; 2a; 3b; 4c; 5c

True or false? 1. false; 2. true; 3. true; 4. false; 5. false; 6. false; 7. true; 8. false

Vocabulary in context: 1c; 2b; 3a; 4c; 5b; 6a; 7a; 8d

Language building

1. *Vocabulary*
Draw attention to the large number of synonyms used: fit, attack, seizure, convulsion, faintness, swimming in the head.
Likewise: passed out/momentary unconsciousness;
came round/came to his senses.
Notice, too, how easy it is to work out the meaning of the word 'flicker' from the variety of contexts in which it occurs.

2. *Linking devices*
What do 'they' (line 2) and 'some' (line 3) refer back to?
What do 'such' (line 5) and 'such' (line 13) refer back to?

Draw attention to the backward-pointing function of these phrases:

in other subjects . . . (line 6)	other than which?
In his case . . . (line 12)	whose case?
. . . more momentum . . . (line 15)	more than what?
. . . in this way . . . (line 17)	in what way?
In another case . . . (line 18)	other than what?
. . . this discovery (line 25)	which discovery?

3. *Idioms*
Draw attention to:
The chances are . . . = probably
There is no way of knowing = nobody knows
To run the risk = to take a risk, to be exposed to danger
4. Draw attention to the precision of the verbs: strangle, clutch, jerk.
Each of them adds layers of meaning to a more general verb: squeeze, hold, move.
Ask students to demonstrate the meaning of these verbs through actions (not too violent in the case of 'strangle', please!)

Summary

Ask students to make a summary of the main points of the passage only, in not more than eight sentences.

Unit 8: Listening comprehension

'A formidable sound'

Professor Gavraud is an engineer who almost gave up his post at an institute in Marseilles because he always felt ill at work. He decided against leaving when he discovered that the recurrent attacks of nausea only worried him when he was in his office at the top of the building. Thinking that there must be something in the room that disturbed him, he tried to track it down with devices sensitive to various chemicals, and even with a Geiger counter, but he found nothing until one day, just as he was about to give up, he leaned back against the wall. The whole room was vibrating at a very low frequency. The source of this energy turned out to be an air-conditioning plant on the roof of the building across the way, and his office was the right shape and the right distance from the machine to resonate in sympathy with it. It was this rhythm, at seven cycles per second, that made him sick.

Fascinated by the phenomenon, Gavraud decided to build machines to produce infrasound so that he could investigate it further. In casting around for likely designs, he discovered that the whistle with a pea in it issued to all French *gendarmes* produced a whole range of low-frequency sounds. So he built a police-whistle 6 feet long and powered it with compressed air. The technician who gave the giant whistle its first trial blast fell down dead on the spot. A post-mortem revealed that all his internal organs had been mashed into a jelly by the vibrations.

Gavraud went ahead with his work more carefully and did the next test out of doors, with all observers screened from the machine in a concrete shelter. When all was ready, they turned the air on slowly – and broke the windows of every building within half a mile of the test site. Later they learnt to control the strength of the infrasound generator more effectively and designed a series of smaller machines for experimental work. One of the most interesting discoveries to date is that waves of low frequency can be aimed, and that two generators focussed on a particular point even five miles away produce a resonance that can knock a building down as effectively as a major earthquake. These frequency-7 machines can be built very cheaply, and plans for them are available for 3 French francs from the Patent Office in Paris.

(From *Supernature* by Lyall Watson)

Answers to 'A formidable sound'

Multiple choice: 1c; 2a; 3d; 4d; 5b

True or false? 1. false; 2. true; 3. false; 4. false; 5. false; 6. true; 7. false; 8. false; 9. false; 10. false; 11. true; 12. false; 13. false

Vocabulary in context: 1b; 2b; 3a; 4b; 5a; 6a; 7b; 8d; 9a

Language building

1. Draw attention to the way in which words and phrases are re-expressed as near-synonyms, e.g.:

he almost *gave up* his post . . . he decided *against* leaving
he *always felt ill* . . . recurrent *fits of nausea*
felt ill/nausea/sick/disturbed him
vibration/resonance/rhythm
trial/test

2. Point out especially the specialised, technical use of some fairly common words, e.g.:

air-conditioning *plant*   *frequency*
internal *organs*   *waves*
in *sympathy*   *cycles*

3. The compound 'air-conditioning' is quite a common formation in English. Other more everyday examples include:
a nerve-racking (experience)
an ear-shattering/ear-splitting (sound)
a hair-splitting (argument)
a money-grubbing (person)
a gold-mining (company)
a labour-saving (gadget/device)

These are all shorthand ways of saying something like this:
a nerve-racking experience = an experience which racks the nerves
a gold-mining company = a company which mines gold

Tell students to watch out for combinations of this kind in their future reading.

4. Draw students' attention to the fact that 'site' means a place, an area, in the open, in which some given act or activity goes on, e.g. a building site, a construction site, an archaeological site, a historical site.

'Site' often occurs in the construction: 'The site of the . . .' e.g. The site of the battle, the site of the landing, etc.

5. *Low-frequency*
Draw attention to the way in which 'low-' and 'high-' enter into compound adjectives of this kind, e.g.:

high/low-pressure (area)   high/low-risk (investment)
high/low-density (housing)   high/low-yield (investment)
high/low-income (group)   high/low-interest (loan)

Expansion exercise

1. Professor Gavraud almost gave up.
2. He decided against leaving . . .
3. He tried to track it down.
4. The room was vibrating.
5. The source turned out to be an air-conditioning plant.
6. It was this that made him sick.
7. Gavraud decided to build machines.
8. He discovered that the whistle produced low-frequency sounds.
9. He built a police whistle.
10. The technician fell down.
11. All his organs had been mashed.
12. Gavraud went ahead more carefully.

13. They turned the air on slowly.
14. They learned to control the infrasound generator.
15. Waves of low-frequency can be aimed.
16. These machines can be built cheaply.

Summary

Now ask students to listen to the tape once more, this time taking brief notes. They should then write out their own version of the passage from their notes.

Unit 9: Reading comprehension

Answers to 'Shaka – King of the Zulus'

Multiple choice: 1c; 2d; 3a; 4c; 5c; 6c

True or false? 1. true; 2. true; 3. true; 4. true; 5. false; 6. false; 7. true

Vocabulary in context: 1c; 2b; 3b; 4b; 5d

Language building

1. *As it was*
This phrase serves here as a conjunction, meaning 'all the same' or 'nevertheless'. The word 'it' may puzzle students because it does not refer to any explicit subject. Expressions in which the function of 'it' cannot be strictly defined are fairly common in English. Remind students of:

as it happened/turned out   what it involves
the way it was   what it means

2. *Sentence* (line 27)
If students cannot deduce the meaning of 'sentence' from the context, ask them to look carefully at these words from the same paragraph:
12,000 warriors *were ordered* . . .
Shaka sent his impis . . . to *punish* . . .
his *orders* for mourning
all women . . . *were to be put to death*

Then ask:
a) Who passed the sentence?
b) Is a *sentence* stronger or weaker than an *order*?
c) Can you refuse to accept a sentence?
d) In everyday life, who is empowered to pass a sentence?

3. *Little less than* (line 27)
This phrase is deceptive. It means, in fact, 'amounted to the same as', 'was equal to'. Other circumlocutions of the same sort commonly used in everyday speech are:
quite a few (many)
not too good (bad)
not bad (not good either)
hardly the right thing to do (the wrong thing to do)

34

4. *Brooding* (line 28)

It is unlikely that students will know the precise meaning of this word (pensive, melancholy, introverted). They should, however, be able to get close to the meaning if they think along these lines:

a) What change came over Shaka after his mother's death?
b) Did he remain as active as he had been before?
c) Why was he 'bitter'?
d) What was he thinking about most of the time?
e) Is bitterness contained in the meaning of brooding?

5. *Gasp* (line 47)

Draw attention to the fact that 'gasp' is always connected, implicitly or explicitly, with words such as: horror, surprise, fear, etc.

6. Inverted word-order occurs frequently in this passage. Ask students to *retell* this story as if to a friend. They should concentrate in particular on reformulating the following sentences:

a) Had Shaka been born in Europe he too might well have altered the course of world affairs (lines 3, 4).
b) And he would have destroyed it had it not been for the courage of a minor chieftain named Gala (lines 5, 6).
c) Only after this had been done did he announce his orders for mourning . . . (lines 22, 23).
d) Total ruin now faced the Zulu nation . . . (line 32).
e) . . . to challenge the King's wishes at such a moment was to ask for instant death (lines 37, 38).
f) That a man should dare to speak to the King in such a way was unthinkable (lines 48, 49).

Discussion

1. Describe Shaka's character with a few well-chosen adjectives.
2. In the first paragraph Shaka is compared with Napoleon. Why?

Unit 9: Listening comprehension

The stamping of the thorns

Shaka's particular genius lay in his great personal attention to detail and in his capacity for hard work. If at all possible, he always insisted on inspecting everything himself, and he invariably checked all reports by getting evidence from as many sources as possible. He was a firm believer in the saying: 'It is the master's eye which makes the cow grow fat.'

Two months after becoming king, Shaka called all his 'regiments' together. His combined fighting forces totalled only about 500 men. He told them of the virtues of the short, heavy stabbing spear or *assegai* which he himself had designed to replace the light throwing one used in the past by the Zulu fighters. As he expected, the younger soldiers took up the new *assegai* with enthusiasm, soon to be followed by the older men.

Next Shaka ordered all his regiments to throw away their sandals. There was considerable protest at this, especially from the older groups, but he pointed to his own bare feet and even ran a race to prove that he was faster than any of his men wearing sandals.

A month later, Shaka noticed that there was still a lot of dissatisfaction and grumbling about his order that sandals should no longer be worn. So, he told one of his regiments to collect many basketsful of the sharp 'devil thorns'. These thorns have three spikes, one of which always points upwards when they lie on the ground.

When enough of these thorns had been collected, Shaka ordered them to be spread over the parade ground. All his regiments were then ordered to parade a little to the side of the ground covered with thorns. Shaka then addressed them: 'It has come to my ears', he said, 'that some of you have soft feet, and this has made me very sad. So I have decided to help you harden them!'

Shaka then ordered his men to stamp the thorns into the ground with their bare feet. Anyone who hesitated or did not stamp hard enough was to be killed at once by his 'slayers'.

The regiments gritted their teeth and, led by Shaka himself, spread over the parade ground. Shaka turned to face them and the stamping began. Shaka's feet, however, were horny and impervious. He felt nothing; but his eagle eye at once picked out those who were hesitant. These men were told to stand forward and were then clubbed to death by the slayers. And so he went on, searching up and down the lines, but after half a dozen examples had been made all the soldiers stamped as hard as they could.

When Shaka was satisfied that the thorns had been stamped out of sight he told his men they could go. That evening they were given a great feast at which they could eat and drink as much as they liked.

(From *Shaka Zulu* by E. A. Ritter)

Answers to 'The stamping of the thorns'

Multiple choice: 1c; 2b; 3c; 4a; 5c

True or false? 1. true; 2. false; 3. true; 4. true; 5. true; 6. false; 7. false; 8. true; 9. true

Vocabulary in context: 1d; 2a; 3c; 4b

Language building

1. *Stamp*
Draw attention to the group of verbs to which 'stamp' belongs. This would include, for example:

tramp	tiptoe (see Unit 18, 'A sunrise on the veld')
march	steal
stride	sneak

2. *Totalled*
(See also the language notes to the Unit 17 Reading comprehension passage 'Our first words'.)
Remind students of other nouns which are often used as verbs in this way, e.g. ranked, figured, topped, averaged.

3. *Gritted their teeth*
Idiomatic expressions connected with parts of the body are common in everyday speech. Here are some worth noting:
to keep one's hand in (= to stay in training, not to lose a skill)
to keep an eye open (= to watch out for something)
to see eye to eye (= to agree on matters of taste/opinion)
to lend a hand (= to help)

Expansion exercise

Ask students to retell the passage freely in their own words, using the following as guidelines:

1. Shaka's genius . . .
2. He insisted on inspecting . . . and . . .
3. He was a firm believer in . . .
4. Shaka called his regiments together.
5. He told them . . .
6. The younger soldiers took up the new *assegai*.
7. Next Shaka ordered his regiments . . .
8. He even ran a race.
9. There was still a lot of dissatisfaction.
10. He told one of his regiments to collect thorns.
11. These thorns have three spikes.
12. When these thorns had been collected . . .
13. All his regiments were ordered to parade.
14. 'Some of you have soft feet.'
15. Shaka then ordered his men . . .
16. Anyone who hesitated was to be killed.
17. The regiments spread over the parade ground.
18. The stamping began.
19. Shaka felt nothing . . . but . . .
20. These men were clubbed to death.
21. After half a dozen examples.
22. When Shaka was satisfied . . .
23. That evening . . .

Discussion

1. Do you think Shaka's methods were cruel? What other great military leaders have used similar methods?
2. Obedience.

Unit 10: Reading comprehension

Answers to 'Packaging'

Multiple choice: 1c; 2a; 3c; 4d; 5d; 6c

True or false? 1. true; 2. false; 3. true; 4. true; 5. false; 6. true; 7. false; 8. false; 9. true; 10. false

Vocabulary in context: 1b; 2a; 3d; 4a; 5a; 6d; 7c; 8b; 9c; 10a

Open-ended questions

1. If most packaging is useless, why is it used?
2. Is packaging in any way a threat to the nation's economy?
3. If paper is to be recycled, who should organise the operation?
4. If paper is to be recycled, why will people need to have separate dustbins?
5. Is it likely that the British dairies will change over completely to using plastic bottles?
6. What worries environmentalists?
7. What does the author mean by 'a sophisticated approach'?

Language building

1. There are certain key-words and notions in this passage. Before students begin reading, they should discuss the topic of 'Packaging'. Try to get them to introduce in their own words the following words and notions:
a) *Waste* – rubbish, refuse, garbage, dustman, dustcart, rubbish-bin, rubbish-disposal, etc.
b) *Wrapping* – packaging, packet, paper, string, glass, cellophane, plastic, bag, etc.
c) *Recycling* – use, re-use, processing, producing, etc.
d) *Environment* – energy, natural resources, disposal (of waste), economy, planning, etc.

2. Focus attention on the language of the first paragraph, particularly the verbs. Notice how much rewording and repetition there is:
to get (an object) *out of* (a box)
unpacking

unpacking
taken out of
torn off
opened
removed
unwrapped

wrapping
done up

Encourage students to imitate physically the motions involved in each of the above words. Where possible, find words meaning the *opposite* of the above.

3. *Prefixes*

Two prefixes are particularly striking in this passage: 're-' and 'un-'. Ask students what they think these two prefixes generally mean. (Re- = again; un- = take off, remove, return to its original state.)

Draw their attention to the following words:

unpacking	recycle
unwrapped	(returned)
	refilled
	(recovery)
	re-use

With the words in brackets, 're-' can no longer be considered a prefix. It has become an integral part of the verb while retaining the meaning of 're-'.

4. *Phrasal verbs*

Ask students to consider the following:

a) *done up in* (line 6). If this means the same as 'wrapped', why did the author choose to use it?

b) *put out* (by) (line 8). What action does this verb describe?

c) *do away with* (lines 30, 31). Is this a synonym for 'abolish'? Does 'do away with' suggest a gradual or a drastic change?

d) *washed out* (line 24). What is the function of *out* in this verb?
(See also the language notes to the Unit 1 Reading comprehension passage, 'Tall tales from the backwoods'.)

5 *Increasingly*

Draw attention to the various ways in which the idea of 'increase' and 'development' is expressed in the passage:
It is now becoming *increasingly difficult* . . . (line 5)
. . . with massive *increases* in paper prices . . . (line 21)
More and more dairies are experimenting (line 25)
. . . the *growing* use of plastic (line 25)
. . . *ever growing* mounds . . . (line 30)
. . . is clearly becoming *increasingly absurd* . . . (lines 36, 37)

Discussion

1. Do you agree that paper should be re-used? Is the author's suggestion for the collection of paper a practical one? What are the difficulties involved in re-collection?
2. What other materials might be profitably re-used?

Recycling waste

Within fifteen years Britain and other nations should be well on with the building of huge industrial complexes for the recycling of waste. The word rubbish could lose its meaning because everything which goes into the dustbin would be made into something useful. Even the most dangerous and unpleasant wastes would provide energy if nothing else.

The new concept of recycling waste is taking shape at the British technological laboratory at Warren Spring, not far north of London. Today; the laboratory spends four times as much money in studying recycling as it did five years ago.

The latest project is to take a city of around half a million inhabitants and discover exactly what raw materials go into it and what go out. The aim is to find out how much of these raw materials could be provided if a plant for recycling waste were built just outside the city. This plant would recycle not only metal such as steel, lead and copper, but also paper and rubber as well. Methods have been discovered, for example, for removing the ink from newsprint so that the paper can be used again, and for obtaining valuable oils and gases from old motor car tyres. All these ideas are already being made use of, but what is new is the idea of combining them on such a large scale in a single plant designed to recycle most types of waste.

Another new project is being set up to discover the best ways of sorting and separating the rubbish. When this project is complete, the rubbish will be processed like this: first, it will pass through sharp metal spikes which will tear open the plastic bags in which rubbish is usually packed; then it will pass through a powerful fan to separate the lightest elements from the heavy solids; after that crushers and rollers will break up everything that can be broken. Finally, the rubbish will pass under magnets, which will remove the bits of iron and steel; the rubber and plastic will then be sorted out in the final stage.

The first full-scale giant recycling plants are, perhaps, fifteen years away. But in some big industrial areas, where rubbish has been dumped for so long that there are no holes left to fill up with rubbish, these new automatic recycling plants may be built sooner. Indeed, with the growing cost of transporting rubbish to more distant dumps, some big cities will be forced to build their own recycling plants before long. (From *Echos de Grande Bretagne*)

Answers to 'Recycling waste'

Multiple choice: 1c; 2c; 3c; 4c

True or false? 1. true; 2. false; 3. false; 4. false; 5. true; 6. false; 7. true; 8. true

Vocabulary in context: 1a; 2b; 3a; 4b; 5b; 6a

Expansion exercise

1. Britain should be well on with the building.
2. Rubbish would lose its meaning.
3. Even . . . wastes would provide energy.
4. The new concept is taking shape.
5. Today, the laboratory spends . . .
6. The latest project is . . .
7. The aim is to find out.

8. This plant would recycle not only . . . but also . . .
9. Methods have been discovered for . . . and for . . .
10. All these ideas are being made use of, but . . .
11. Another new project . . .
12. The rubbish will be processed. like this: first . . . then . . . after that.
13. Finally . . .
14. . . . in the final stage.
15. The first plants are fifteen years away.
16. In some industrial areas there are no holes.
17. Indeed . . . some cities will be forced . . .

Language building

1. *Expressions of time*

Draw attention to:

within fifteen years
five years ago
when . . . is complete
. . . dumped for so long
before long
today
are already being made use of
fifteen years away
may be built sooner

These phrases will prove useful for practising *tenses.*

2. *Tenses*

The range of tenses in this passage is remarkably wide. Notice, in particular:

a) the contrast between present simple and present continuous:
Today, the laboratory *spends* . . .
The new concept *is taking shape*

b) The combination of present and future after *when*:
When this project *is* complete . . . the rubbish *will* pass . . .

c) The frequent use of the passive voices:
would be made into
could be provided
have been discovered
are already being made use of   etc.

d) The use of 'could', 'would' and 'should' for predictions:
Britain *should* be well on with the building . . .
The word rubbish *could* lose its meaning . . .
Even the most dangerous wastes *would* provide energy . . .

3. *Vocabulary*

Note the recurrence of words that appeared in the Reading comprehension passage, e.g.

recycle
separate
remove
(raw) materials
process

and of expressions or words that are practically synonymous:
rubbish/refuse/waste
plant/machine
sort/separate
studying/research
crush/pulp

4. Constructions commonly associated with certain nouns such as 'method', 'way', 'idea' . . .
methods . . . *for removing*
methods . . . *for obtaining*
(the) idea *of combining* them
(the best) ways *of sorting* and *separating*

Other nouns which take similar constructions are: means, chance, plan, system, hope, thought, etc. in expressions such as:
no *means of exploiting* the material
no *chance of getting* your money back
a plan for improving the roads
a *system for operating* the lights
little *hope of making* him change his mind
the *thought of leaving* is absurd

Unit 11:   Reading comprehension

Answers to 'How lions hunt'

Multiple choice: 1d; 2c; 3d; 4b

True or false? 1. false; 2. false; 3. false; 4. false; 5. false; 6. false

Vocabulary in context: 1c; 2c; 3c; 4a; 5d

Language building

1. Notice how often the writer uses '-ing' forms of the verb for the sake of economy:
Setting off at dusk . . . (line 2)
. . . with lionesses *busy hunting*, the males function as guards for the cubs, *protecting*
them . . . (lines 5–6)
. . . a lioness pulls her prey down *after running up* behind it, and then seizes it by the
throat, *strangling* it (lines 13–14)
Sighting prey, lionesses usually fan out . . . (lines 16–17)
A lioness has *no trouble pulling down* an animal . . . (line 29)
. . . the buffalo *whirling* round to face the cat . . . (line 31)
. . . *intent*, it seemed, *on committing* suicide (line 35)
. . . *without trying* to defend himself (lines 36–7)

First, get the students to re-read these sentences in context. Then ask them to explain
what has been said in their own words, avoiding as far as possible the use of the phrases
in italics. Remember that in the spoken language such constructions are often replaced
by the infinitive with 'to' ('a lioness finds it quite easy to pull down . . .') or by an
adverb + verb ('when they set off at dusk on a hunt'.)

Second, practise these three forms in other combinations:
a) busy hunting (i.e. busy + -ing)
b) no trouble pulling down (trouble + -ing)
c) without trying (try + -ing)

Here are some suggestions:
a) busy fixing a fuse, when . . .
   busy making up the final list, when . . .
   busy getting the tickets while . . .
   busy trying to find out what . . .
   busy getting ready for . . .

b) no trouble finding the way
  no trouble (in) getting through to London last night
  no trouble crossing the border
  no trouble getting the wheel changed

c) without wanting
  without realising
  without knowing
  without asking
  without stopping

2. Draw attention to the vivid use of verbs in this passage:

a) *Verbs of movement*	b) *Verbs of action*
lag (behind)	grab
fan (out)	slap
stalk	pull down
scatter	seize
bolt	down (*downed*)
backtrack	
circle	
wander	
plod	
sink	
crouch	

Mention, also, the way in which these two verbs are formed: to down (*downed*); to backtrack.

Give other examples of verbs formed either directly from prepositions or by attaching the preposition to the verb as a prefix, e.g.:

to round (the bend)	to backdate
to near (the shore)	to backfire
to up ('prices have been upped')	to backslide
to down (a beer)	to backpedal

3. Draw attention to the use of 'would' (lines 27–32)
. . . several lionesses *would* sit and wait . . .
. . . then they *would* spread out and advance . . .
. . . having learnt that the gazelle *would not* try to escape . . .

Point out that it is the word 'often' ('One pride of lions often pursued prey') which, in fact, determines the structure of the sentences to follow. Remind students that this use of 'would' to describe habitual past actions is particularly common after words such as:

sometimes	occasionally
usually	seldom
often	never

4. *Blend*
Notice how the meaning of this word is revealed gradually through the context:
Lionesses have learnt to take advantage of their environment . . .
Darkness provides them with *cover* . . .
At *dusk* . . . they wait . . . until their outlines *blend into* the surroundings.

The student should have no difficulty in working out the exact meaning of 'blend'.
If necessary, however, ask him:
a) When hunting at dusk do the lionesses move or stay still?
b) Why do they stay still?
c) Does the light get stronger or weaker at dusk? etc.

5. *Prey* and *quarry*

These are synonyms, though 'prey' is more frequently used than 'quarry'. If students
have difficulty with the words draw their attention to the second paragraph. Here the
names of different animals, and the word 'animal' as well, are in a sense synonymous
with prey. Ask students:
a) Can any animal be a prey?
b) Can a lion be the prey of a gazelle? Can a cat be the prey of a mouse?

6. *Muzzle* and *suffocate*

These two words are logically connected. Try to get students to decide how the lion
could kill its prey in this way What part of the animal's body could be small enough
for the lion to 'place its mouth over'? If 'muzzle' means 'nose', what will happen to the
animal when the lion covers its muzzle?

7. *Slothfulness*

Notice the clues that are given to the meaning of this word:
reticent about spending their energy
walking slowly . . . as if they were bored
bring up the rear

8. *Survival value*

Point out other expressions in which 'value' appears in this way.

snob value	entertainment value
publicity value	social value
education value	commercial value

9. *Belly-deep*

Compounds with 'high' and 'deep' are commonly associated with parts of the body, e.g.:
ankle-deep; waist-deep; knee-high; chest-deep.

Notice, also, the use of 'up to', e.g.: up to my ears (in work); up to my eyes;
up to the elbow; up to his chin.

Open-ended questions

1. Are male lions really lazy?
2. Why do lionesses like to hunt in the evening?
3. What techniques does a lion use when attacking animals larger than itself?
4. In what way does the 'cooperative hunting technique' of lions resemble techniques
of human warfare?
5. Explain how the lionesses trap gazelle near streams.
6. Does the lion fear the buffalo?

How lions live

Males and females play very different roles in lion society. Lionesses stay together for life, except for a few young ones who leave the pride to wander alone. But males are only temporary members.

The life of a male is insecure. Fewer than 10 per cent reach old age. Three-quarters die violently, caught in traps, shot by hunters, or killed in fights with others of their kind. Membership of a pride is a form of life insurance, in that each animal can keep itself alive from kills made by others. With few exceptions, old males lack such membership, and slowly starve to death, watched by vultures and hyenas.

Each pride confines itself to a definite territory, in which strangers are usually not welcome. Intruders are chased with much roaring, but often the pursuers take care not to run fast enough to catch anyone. This is not always the case. I once found a male lion covered in blood, lying on the ground and breathing with difficulty. Suddenly a huge lion came out of the bush, walked up to the lion on the ground and gazed down at him triumphantly. Then he returned to the remains of a zebra over which they had probably been fighting, and left the lion on the ground to die.

The death of that male gave me a deeper insight into the complexity of lion society. After his death, the males from three other prides penetrated his former territory and drove out his companion. Three cubs were pursued and bitten to death. A further three were killed; two were carried off. I waited by the remaining cub for the return of its mother. I was not certain what to expect; certainly not a terrible explosion of grief, but maybe some sentiment. In fact she ate the cub. I sat in the dark listening to her crunch the bones.

Lions are self-indulgent, and seldom permit the needs of cubs to conflict with their own desires. When adult lions tear apart the carcass of a dead animal they fiercely defend their portions. It is depressing to see a starving cub turn to its mother for food and receive a vicious blow instead of a bite to eat.

Cubs always manage to obtain a meal from a large carcass if they are present when a kill is made, but if they are waiting in the bush for their mother's return they may not be so lucky. Only after the lioness has gorged herself is she likely to fetch her cubs. By the time she has done so there may be no meat left. But the males occasionally come to the rescue. While eating together with the lionesses, they may suddenly drive them off the carcass. Cubs are then permitted to join them, and in this way are often provided with a meal.

(From *Serengeti, a Kingdom of Predators* by George Schaller)

Answers to 'How lions live'

Multiple choice: 1b; 2a; 3c; 4d

True or false? 1. true; 2. true; 3. false; 4. true; 5. true; 6. false; 7. false; 8. true; 9. false; 10. false

Vocabulary in context: 1b; 2d; 3a; 4a; 5b; 6b; 7c; 8a; 9a; 10a

Language building

1. The article
Notice how frequently the article ('a' or 'the') is omitted both in this passage and in the Reading comprehension text. Draw attention, particularly, to the following:
Males and females play very different roles . . .
But *males* are only temporary members . . .
Membership of a pride . . .
. . . *old males* lack such membership . . .
Intruders are chased . . .
the needs of *cubs* . . .
Cubs always manage to obtain . . .

Now consider these phrases in which an article is used:
The life of *a* male . . .
. . . often *the* pursuers take care . . .
. . . *the* males from three other prides . . .
But *the* males occasionally come to the rescue . . .
While eating together with *the* lionesses . . .

Notice that in many cases the use or omission of the article is arbitrary (e.g. *intruders* are chased . . . *the* pursuers take care). What general principle can be drawn from these examples?

2. Self-indulgent
Compounds with 'self-' as a prefix are common in English. Remind students that when referring to a person, 'self-' often has a pejorative meaning, as in: self-satisfied; self-centred; self-assured

There are, however, compounds in which 'self-' is neutral, e.g. self-made; self-taught; self-sufficient

'Self-' need not always refer to a person. Remind students of the following:
self-contained (flat); self-raising (flour); self-sealing (envelope); self-destroying (material); self-governing (organisation)

3. Pride is a group noun. Such words are less common, perhaps, than certain grammarians would have us think. Nevertheless, some are worth noting:
swarm (of bees, locusts, ants, etc. See also Unit 18)
flock   (of birds, sheep)
herd   (of cattle, zebras, elephants)
pack   (of wolves, dogs)

Discussion

1 What other animals belong to the same family as the lion?
2 Where do they live? What are their distinguishing characteristics?
3 Do you think that the hunting of wild animals for their furs should be forbidden?

Unit 12: Reading comprehension

Answers to 'Uri Geller's extraordinary powers'

Multiple choice: 1d; 2d; 3a; 4d; 5c

True or false? 1. false; 2. true; 3. true; 4. false; 5. false; 6. true; 7. false; 8. false; 9. false

Vocabulary in context: 1c; 2c; 3b; 4a; 5b; 6b

Open-ended questions

1. What is meant by 'telepathy'?
2. How was it possible for the scientists to record the effects of Uri's concentration on the metal ring?
3. Why did the experiment with Uri disturb the computers?
4. What was the purpose of the experiments with the drawings in sealed envelopes and the dice?
5. What is the attitude of the author of this passage towards Uri Geller? Is he sceptical, neutral, or passionately enthusiastic?

Language building

1. The following verbs have many different meanings in English: do, go, make, get.

Ask students to replace them with other verbs in the following sentences:
a) Uri first *did* five tests of telepathy . . . (line 1)
b) The copper ring had *gone* from a circle to an egg-shape (line 6)
c) The entire procedure was recorded by sound waves which *made* a picture similar to an X-ray . . . (lines 17–18)
d) The experiments *went on* for five weeks (line 26)
e) He admitted that he could not *get* about one in five of the drawings . . . (lines 29–30)

2. *Deflected*
Students may not know the exact meaning of this word. They should, however, be able to make a reasonably accurate guess from the context. If necessary, ask the following questions:
Is deflection a fixed state or a movement?
What is the usual meaning of the prefix *de-*?
What was Uri Geller trying to do?
Did he succeed?

48

Draw attention to other words which contain the prefix 'de-' meaning 'off' or 'away from', e.g.:

derailed (a train, a tram)	deluded
deprived	dethroned
deported	detour
deposed	demobilisation

3. Draw attention to the heavy use of the passive voice in this text. Pick out, in particular, those passive constructions commonly used in semi-scientific writing for the sake of objectivity, e.g.:
it was observed (that)
it was noticed (that)
it was seen (that)
should not be interpreted (as proof)
(See also the language notes to the Units 16 and 20, Reading comprehension passage, 'Population growth and industry' and 'The dangers of space'.)

4. *Videotaped*
With the growth of technology, such verbs derived from nouns are becoming increasingly common in English. Ask students which of the following nouns can be used as verbs. (Those which have no verbal form are marked with an asterisk.)

typewriter★	tape-recorder
iron	cassette★
film	telegram/cable
telex	telephone
microphone★	stapler★
television★	photocopier★
radio	spin-drier

Note: most of the nouns ending in '-er' do have a similar verb form, e.g. tape-recorder, to tape-record.
'Typewriter' is an exception. The participle 'typewritten' is common, but there is no verb 'to typewrite'.

Discussion

1. Discuss the precise meaning of words closely connected with the subject of 'telepathy', e.g. perception, intuition, transmission, psyche, illusion, interference, etc.

2. Can you give any examples of everyday occurrences of telepathy? Draw upon your personal experience, but try, wherever possible, to explain what happened.

3. What is the meaning of remarks such as:
Speak of the Devil and he's sure to appear
Just the man I wanted to see!
Funny you should say that . . .

Telepathy

Let us now consider a modern case of telepathy. A girl of about ten years of age was walking along a country lane, reading a book on geometry. Quite suddenly her surroundings seemed to fade away, and she saw her mother lying apparently dead on the floor of a little-used room at home, known as the 'white room'. Near her on the floor was a handkerchief. The child was so upset by this vision that instead of going straight home she rushed to the doctor's house and persuaded him to go home with her. They found the woman lying on the floor of the 'white room' suffering from a severe heart attack. Beside her was the handkerchief. The doctor arrived in time to save her life.

The case is a good one. The story is not one that a child of ten would be expected to invent in a crisis. Moreover, it was verified that she did visit the doctor before going home. Quite possibly, however, the tale was 'helped' by the addition of details after the event. The mention of the handkerchief may have been added later to make the story sound more impressive, or it may even have been a distortion of memory. What is most important is that the child acted on her vision and went straight to the doctor.

Quite recently in the *New York Times* Magazine a physician tried to discredit the case by suggesting that the child's mother may have been an hysteric who frequently imagined she was having heart attacks, and so there would be nothing very remarkable in the child's inventing a vision of her parent suffering from such a seizure. The suggestion does not seem very likely. Had the woman been subject to such attacks, genuine or imagined, the doctor would surely have mentioned the fact. Moreover, later in her life the girl frequently spoke about the incident as something unique in her experience, which she would scarcely have done had the vision been a mere exercise of the imagination.

(From *Modern Experiments in Telepathy* by Soal and Bateman)

Answers to 'Telepathy'

Multiple choice: 1b; 2d; 3b; 4c; 5b

True or false? 1. false; 2. false; 3. true; 4. true; 5. false; 6. false; 7. true; 8. false; 9. false; 10. false; 11. true

Vocabulary in context: 1b; 2a; 3b; 4c; 5d; 6b; 7c

Language building

1. Point out the emphatic use of 'did' in: 'Moreover, it was verified that she *did* visit the doctor . . .'

'Did' is used in this way whenever the speaker or writer wishes:
a) to counter a criticism, doubt, or objection (even if it is not explicit, as here)
b) to justify an action (e.g. I *did* try to warn him, but . . .)
c) to confirm an assumption/question (e.g. 'He did pay you, didn't he? – Yes, he *did*')

2. Notice the various ways in which the speaker avoids repeating the same noun in any single sentence:

a) by using 'one':
The case is a good *one*.
The story is not *one* that a child of ten . . .

b) by using synonyms:
. . . the child's *mother* = . . . her *parent*
. . . having heart *attacks* = . . . suffering from such a *seizure*
. . . the *incident* . . . = . . . the *vision*

c) by omission
. . . the *suggestion* does not seem very likely (i.e. instead of 'a very likely one')
. . . such *attacks* . . . genuine or imagined . . .

3. Draw attention to the last paragraph of the passage, in which various suggestions are discussed. Notice the language the speaker uses to bring out his point of view:
The suggestion does not seem very likely.
Had the woman been subject to such attacks . . . the doctor would surely have mentioned the fact.
Moreover . . . which she would scarcely have done had the vision . . .

Notice, too, the frequent use of 'may have been':
The mention of the handkerchief *may have been added later* . . .
. . . or it *may have been* a distortion of memory.
. . . the child's mother *may have been* an hysteric . . .

Expansion exercise

1. Let us consider a case.
2. A girl was walking.
3. Quite suddenly . . . she saw her mother.
4. Near her . . .
5. The child was upset.
6. She rushed to the doctor.
7. They found the woman.
8. The doctor arrived in time.
9. The story is not one . . .
10. It was verified . . .
11. The tale was 'helped' by the addition of details.
12. The handkerchief may have been added later.
13. What is most important is . . .
14. Quite recently a physician tried . . . by suggesting that . . .
15. There would be nothing very remarkable . . .
16. Had the woman . . . the doctor would surely . . .
17. Moreover, later in her life . . .
18. . . . which she would scarcely have done . . .

Discussion and summary

1. Play the tape again. Now ask students to retell the story in not more than six sentences.
2. Is it possible to 'see' events happening before they take place?

Unit 13: Reading comprehension

Answers to 'Battery buses'

Multiple choice: 1b; 2d; 3a; 4a; 5c

True or false? 1. false; 2. false; 3. false; 4. false; 5. false; 6. true; 7. true; 8. true; 9. true; 10. false

Vocabulary in context: 1b; 2d; 3a; 4d; 5c

Open-ended questions

1. Why is the government-sponsored bus not so useful as the Silent Rider?
2. What reasons might make us prefer battery buses?
3. What are the main advantages of the Mark II over the prototype?

Language building

1. Ask students to look through the passage to identify all the ways in which the bus is referred back to (a battery-driven bus, the prototype, a fifty-passenger single-deck vehicle, the new Silent Rider, a larger, Mark II version, it.)

2. *Greater operational flexibility* . . . refers back to a fact mentioned in the previous paragraph, namely that the prototype is somewhat lacking in flexibility because it takes three and a half hours to recharge. Encourage students to make this inference for themselves by asking them which fact is being referred back to.

A similar general way of saying something which is made explicit elsewhere occurs in two other instances:

General	*Specific*
. . . environmental benefits	quiet and pollution-free
competitive . . . on cost and performance	. . . lower maintenance and fuel costs . . . competitive cost

Give students the general statements and ask them to identify the specific ones.

3. The passage is rich in hyphenated compound adjectives:
battery-driven
government-sponsored
pollution-free
low-cost
fifty-passenger

Draw attention to these and try to elicit further examples of other similarly formed compounds, e.g.:
home-made (cake)
remote-controlled (missile)
power-drunk (leader)
top-heavy (organisation)
high-fidelity (equipment)
quick-service (bar)
64,000-dollar (question)
two-seater (car)

4. Draw attention to 'recharged'.
'Re-' is, of course, one of the most useful prefixes in English (see Unit 13, Listening comprehension passage 'Atomic cars'), since it can be applied to many verbs, changing the meaning to 'do again', e.g.: he made his bed; he re-made his bed. Try to elicit further examples from the students.

Prototype
'proto-' is a less useful prefix, but it is found a good deal in scientific texts (e.g. protoplasm, protozoa, etc.)

5. Two group nouns are used in the passage: 'batch' and 'set'. 'Set' is much more common and can be applied to a great many things, e.g.: a tea set, a model-railway set, a chess-set, a set of tools, a set of paints, a set of instruments.

Elicit examples of 'sets'. They are nearly always things which are intended to be kept together for ever.

'Batch' is rather unusual. Again it refers to a group of things all together. Usually there is an idea of their having been produced together or of their being sent somewhere together. The members of a 'batch' are identical; those of a 'set' belong together but are not necessarily identical.

Unit 13: Listening comprehension

Atomic cars

Every motorist dreams of a car of the future that does not have to be refuelled every few hundred miles, a car that will cost little to run because there is no outlay on petrol.

'Of course', you hear it said by an optimistic motorist, 'the answer is the atom. Harness atomic power in a car, and you'll have no more worries about petrol. The thing will run for years without a refill.'

And, theoretically, he is right. The answer is the atom. If atomic power could be used in a car, one small piece of uranium would keep the engine running for twenty or more years. Of course, this would cut the cost of running a car by quite a few hundred pounds, depending upon how much you spend on petrol.

But is this science-fiction-like picture of the atom exploding peacefully beneath the bonnet of a car possible? In theory it is, since already the atom has been harnessed to drive submarines, and an atomic engine is already in existence. But, say the experts, there are many problems still to be conquered before such an engine can in fact be fixed into a car.

Now what exactly are these problems that stand between you and a car that you will never have to refuel? Frankly, most of them can be summed up in one word – radiation. An atomic reactor, the kind of engine that would produce energy by atom-splitting, throws off radiation, extremely dangerous radiation. These rays are just as dangerous as when they are released from an atomic bomb. This radiation penetrates anything except the thickest concrete and lead, with fatal results for anybody in its path. Thus, at the moment, any car carrying an atomic engine would also have to carry many tons of lead in order to prevent the radiation from escaping.

Since a car made up of tons of lead is rather impracticable, the only answer at the moment seems to be the discovery or invention of a metal that will be strong enough to hold in the rays, but at the same time light enough for a vehicle to carry with ease and economy. Most likely this metal would have to be synthetic, since no natural metal except lead has yet proved fit for the job. When this light metal is invented, the motoring world will be well on the way to an atomic car. However, even after the invention of a protective but light metal, two other problems still remain, those of economics and safety.

It is extremely doubtful whether at the beginning a really economic engine could be made, that is, one cheap enough to make it worth putting in a car. But it seems safe to say that eventually, as techniques and mass production come in atomic engines, the price will go down. This is basic economics, and manufacturers should eventually be able to produce something that will at least be cheaper than having to pay for petrol during the lifetime of the car.

But then this third problem still remains, that of safety. Suppose that there is a road accident involving one, or perhaps two, atomic cars, and that the atomic reactor or its protective covering were damaged. Any explosion would be equal to that of a very small atomic bomb. The effects of such an explosion would be felt for several miles around. As will be realised, this is perhaps the biggest problem of all to overcome. Is it possible to make an atomic engine that will be really safe in every circumstance?

(From an article in *Ford Times*)

Answers to 'Atomic cars'

Multiple choice: 1d; 2d; 3d; 4a; 5d

True or false? 1. false; 2. true; 3. false; 4. true; 5. true; 6. false; 7. false

Vocabulary in context: 1d; 2a; 3c; 4d; 5b; 6a

Language building

1. Play the sentence: 'This is basic economics . . . the lifetime of the car.' Then ask students to look for a comparable section in the Reading comprehension passage. ('Its capital cost . . . over a thirteen-year life.')

2. Draw attention, by stopping the tape at the appropriate points, to the way in which certain key facts and ideas are referred to repeatedly, often in slightly different ways, e.g.:

radiation
dangerous radiation
These rays are just as dangerous . . .
. . . this radiation penetrates . . .
. . . prevent the radiation . . .
. . . hold in the rays . . .

invention of a metal
. . . this metal . . .
. . . this light metal . . .
. . . a protective but light metal . . .

a car that will cost little to run
. . . run for years without a refill . . .
. . . keep the engine running for twenty or more years . . .
. . . cut the cost of running a car.

3. Show how certain apparently difficult words or phrases are often explained by the words which follow them, e.g.:
An *atomic reactor*, the *kind of engine that* . . .
. . . a really *economic* engine, that is, one *cheap enough* . . .

4. Remind students of the usefulness of the prefix 're-' (refuelled, refill, etc.) and of the usefulness of such compounds as 'outlay' and 'overcame'.
(See also language notes to the Reading comprehension Units 1, 14, 19: 'Tall tales from the backwoods', 'Shape and waves', and 'The secrets of sleep'.)

5. *Synthetic*
The prefix 'syn-' is of some use in guessing at meaning, especially as it also occurs as 'sym-', e.g.:

synthetic	sympathy
synchronise	symphony
synonym	symmetrical
syndrome	symbiosis
synopsis	
syntax	

It has the general meaning of 'bringing together, coming together, or belonging together'.
Hence *synthesis* = the bringing together of separate elements to form a new one.

6. *Harness*
A good example of a noun transformed into a verb. Try to elicit other examples, e.g.:
to hammer, to knife, to screw, to paper, to pitchfork, etc.

Expansion exercise

1. Every motorist dreams.
2. You hear it said.
3. Harness atomic power.
4. He is right.
5. Uranium would keep the engine running.
6. This would cut the cost.
7. Is this possible?

8. The atom has been harnessed.
9. There are many problems.
10. What are these problems?
11. One word.
12. An atomic reactor throws off radiation.
13. These rays are just as dangerous.
14. This radiation penetrates anything.
15. Any car would have to carry lead.
16. The only answer seems to be a metal that will be strong but light.
17. This metal would be synthetic.
18. Two other problems remain.
19. It is doubtful.
20. The price will go down.
21. This is basic economics.
22. This third problem remains.
23. Suppose that there is a road accident.
24. Any explosion would be equal to a bomb.
25. This is the biggest problem.
26. Is it possible?

Open-ended questions

1. Thinking back on both reading and listening passages, what do you consider are the reasons for wanting to find alternatives to conventional vehicles?
2. What makes atomic cars a risky undertaking?
3. Which are the three major problems in the way of atomic cars?

Discussion

1. At the moment the industrialised world depends on petrol. What are the alternatives, if any?
2. What would be your reaction if the government proposed to build a nuclear (atomic) power-station near your home?
3. What do you think is the long-term solution to the world's energy problem? (See, for example, the reports of the Club of Rome.)

Unit 14 Reading comprehension

Answers to 'Shape and waves'

Multiple choice: 1c; 2c; 3b; 4c; 5b

True or false? 1. false; 2. false; 3. true; 4. false; 5. false; 6. true; 7. false; 8. true; 9. false; 10. true

Vocabulary in context: 1. enhanced   2. same, different and differing   3a; 4d; 5b; 6d; 7a; 8b; 9a; 10a

11 a) corkscrew pattern
   b) radiating wheel-spokes
   c) concentric circles (annular rings)
   d) waves that run in lines
   e) vanishing spirals
   f) hexagonal grids
   g) trapezoidal
   h) alternating lines
   i) spherical
   j) round barrels

Language building

1. The passage is full of words describing shape, or used in connection with shape.
Some are familiar: round, rings, forms, shape, pattern, line, arrangement, figures.
Others less familiar: angular, spherical, spiral, corkscrew, grid, concentric.
Others very specialised: trapezoidal, hexagonal.
Ask students to identify all the words in the passage which have to do with *shape*.

2. There are one or two specialised words or phrases which may need a word of explanation:
micro-organism = some sort of bacteria
schizophrenic   = mental patient suffering from 'split personality'
manta ray = a large flat fish
DNA = the 'stuff of life', the chemical which transmits hereditary characteristics in the chromosomes.
Before explaining, however, try to extract the meaning from students by deduction.

3. *Updraught*
Draw attention to this compound and to common related words using the same prefix, e.g.: *up*wards; an *up*rush/*up*surge; to *up*hold; an *up*rising; to/an *up*set.

4. *Wind-blown*
This is another familiar way of forming compounds in English:
wind-blown = blown by the wind.
Draw attention to other common compounds of the same form: man-made (hand-made)
sunburnt, gas-heated, heaven-sent, fascist-inspired, windswept, home-grown etc.
(See also Unit 5, Reading comprehension passage, 'Oil wealth flows up the Voe'.)

5. physicist – physics
   architect – architecture
   researcher – research
Draw attention to the way the noun describing the practitioner derives from the noun
describing the subject he practises.

6. Draw attention to the formation of the following:
muscul*ar* (from muscle)
angul*ar* (from angle)
particul*ar* (from particle)
famili*ar* (from family)

Ask students to form adjectives in the same way from the following:

circle	triangle
single	tube
vehicle	spectacle
rectangle	

Then study the formation of these adjectives:

environmen*tal*	and:	spheri*cal* (sphere)
trapezoid*al*		identi*cal* (identity)
hexagon*al*		
spir*al*		
function*al*		
tropi*cal*		

Ask students to form adjectives in the same way for the following:

regular		*irregular*
detriment	topic	commerce
experiment	logic	part
incident	magic	horizon
president	lyric	sex
sentiment		contract

Unit 14: Listening comprehension

What happens inside a pyramid?

The pyramids on the west bank of the Nile were built by the pharaohs as royal tombs
and date from about 3000 B.C. The most celebrated are those at Giza, of which the
largest is the one that housed the pharaoh known as Cheops. This is now called the
Great Pyramid. Some years ago it was visited by a Frenchman named Bovis, who took
shelter from the midday sun in the pharaoh's chamber, which is situated in the centre

of the pyramid, exactly one third of the way up from the base. He found it unusually humid there, but what really surprised him were the garbage cans that contained, among the usual tourist litter, the bodies of a cat and some small desert animals that had wandered into the pyramid and died there. Despite the humidity, none of them had decayed, but just dried out like mummies. He began to wonder whether the pharaohs had really been so carefully embalmed by their subjects after all, or whether there was something about the pyramids themselves that preserved bodies in a mummified condition.

Bovis made an accurate scale model of the Cheops pyramid and placed it, like the original, with the base lines facing precisely north–south and east–west. Inside the model, one third of the way up, he put a dead cat. It became mummified, and he concluded that the pyramid causes rapid dehydration. Reports of this discovery attracted the attention of Karel Drbal, a radio engineer in Prague, who repeated the experiment with several dead animals and concluded, 'There is a relation between the shape of the space inside the pyramid and the physical, chemical and biological processes going on inside that space. By using suitable forms and shapes, we should be able to make processes occur faster or to delay them.'

Drbal remembered an old superstition which said that a razor left in the light of the moon became blunted. He tried putting one under his model pyramid, but nothing happened, so he went on shaving with it until it was blunt, and then put it back in the pyramid. It became sharp again.

I tried keeping the same objects – eggs, rump-steak, dead mice – in both a pyramid and an ordinary shoe-box, and the ones in the model pyramid preserved quite well while those in the box soon began to smell and had to be thrown out. I am forced to conclude that a cardboard replica of the Cheops pyramid is not just a random arrangement of pieces of paper, but does have special properties.
(From *Supernature* by Lyall Watson)

Answers to 'What happens inside a pyramid'

Multiple choice: 1d; 2b; 3c; 4b; 5c; 6c; 7c

True or false? 1. false; 2. false; 3. true; 4. false; 5. false; 6. true; 7. false; 8. true; 9. false; 10. false; 11. false; 12. true

Vocabulary in context: 1b; 2b; 3d; 4c; 5a; 6b; 7a; 8: that he has a cold; 9d; 10b; 11b

Language building

Draw attention to the following devices in word-formation:
1. *De*hydration. The prefix 'de-' nearly always means 'to deprive of', 'to take away from'. Hence dehydration = taking away the water from something, drying out.

The device is frequently used in scientific and journalistic writing, e.g.:

decarbonise	defuse
desulphurise	depopulate
deodorise	depose
depolarise	derail

2. *Humid* forms its noun: humi*dity*. A number of other nouns behave identically: stupid, timid, avid, sordid, morbid, etc.

Students should not, however, assume that all adjectives ending in '-id' form nouns in '-idity', e.g.:
splendid – splendour
torpid   – torpor
candid   – candour

3. The verb 'mummify' is formed from the noun 'mummy' in the passage. The suffix '-ify' means to 'take on the characteristics of' or 'to carry out the process of'. Here are some further examples:

solidify	falsify
identify	intensify
beautify	verify

There are other verbal suffixes which have a similar meaning. One is '-ate': dehydrate, stagnate, aerate, separate, isolate, aggravate, populate.

Also '-ise' (or '-ize'): magnetise, advertise, pulverise, tenderise, vulcanise.

4. Draw attention to the structure:
he tried –ing (something)
He tried putting one under his model . . .
I tried keeping the same objects . . .
Whenever 'try' is followed by the '-ing' form it means 'to make an experiment'. Whenever it occurs with 'to', e.g. 'I tried to climb the wall', it means 'to make an attempt'.

5. *Base*
Work on the meaning of 'base' by asking:
Is it a point or an area?
Is it at the top or at the bottom?
Does it support a weight or not?

Open-ended questions

1. How many people carried out experiments with model pyramids?
2. What surprised Bovis about the condition of the dead animals in the Great Pyramid?
3. What did he do to check his suspicions?
4. Why did Drbal put a razor-blade inside his model pyramid?
5. What did the speaker do to check on these ideas?

Discussion

1. Do you believe what you have just heard? How could you test it?
2. Is there a connection between what you read and what you heard? Try to recall as many of the facts from both passages as you can.
3. Think of some common objects. Is there any reason for their being the shape they are?

Unit 15: Reading comprehension

Answers to 'Lost world of the Kalahari'

Multiple choice: 1c; 2a; 3d; 4c; 5b; 6d; 7a; 8d

True or false? 1. false; 2. false; 3. true; 4. false; 5. false; 6. true; 7. true; 8. false; 9. false; 10. false; 11. false; 12. true; 13. true

Vocabulary in context: 1c; 2c; 3c; 4c; 5d; 6c; 7a; 8b

Open-ended questions

1. Who fired the shots?
2. Why did the writer feel guilty?
3. Why did he forget to tell his friends about his promise?
4. Why did Samutchoso want nothing to be killed near the hills?
5. What was so strange about the hills?
6. What did the writer imagine as he came down from the hills?
7. What do you think the connection is between these two moments?
   'My blood went cold within me' (line 5)
   '. . . the hair slowly creeping at the back of my neck' (line 44)
8. What do you think happens next?

Language building

1. Draw attention to the compounds 'overlaid' and 'overlooked'.
Try to elicit other words formed in the same way, e.g.: overcome, overwhelm, overtake, oversee. Here it means something like 'on top of', 'from above'.

Draw attention to the other meaning of 'over' in compounds, e.g. overeat, oversleep, over-estimate, overpay, over-excite. Here it means 'too much'.

Note the compound 'afterglow'. Again elicit further analogous examples, e.g. after-effects, aftermath, after-taste.

2. Note the following:
. . . an acute sense of guilt
. . . a sense of mystery.

The construction 'a sense of . . .' is often used instead of an adjective, e.g.: I had a sense of guilt = I felt guilty

Other common nouns associated with 'a sense of . . .' are:
humour
timing/time
duty
economy
proportion

3. It is worth pointing out the following useful idiomatic phrases:
couldn't have been more than . . .
would have been welcome . . .
in the hope that . . .
it was just as bad . . .

4. If there is time, attention should be drawn to some of the features which mark the style of this passage.
a) The brilliance of the opening paragraph: 'a dazzle of zebra' instead of just 'a herd of zebra'. The image of the ostrich as a ballet dancer. The precision of 'snapped the tense silence'.

b) The large number of words which relate to inner feelings rather than to external acts, e.g. sense, instinct, within me, within him, etc.

c) The rôle of words like: soar, lift, rise.

d) The extended metaphor 'stir . . . bowl'.

e) The author's preference for words of Latin origin in many cases, e.g.: extracted, devotion, essential, conducted, communicate, installed, etc.,

and for slightly archaic, even Biblical, turns of phrase, e.g.: 'My blood . . . within me' instead of 'inside me' or even just 'my blood went cold'.

5. *Snapped*
Work over the field of meaning of 'snap':
Is it a sharp or a dull noise?
Is it a long or a short noise?
Is it produced by tension or by pressure?
What is involved as well as the noise?
Is it a sudden, clean break?
What sort of things commonly snap? (e.g. a twig, a rope, a cable)

6. *Disembowelling*
Which animals were in fact shot? From this it should be clear what sort of an action 'disembowelling' is. If John and Jeremiah were doing something to a dead animal, they must have been either skinning, cleaning the insides, cooking or eating it. Cooking and eating can be excluded. And for the overall meaning of the text it does not much matter which of the other two alternatives we understand, although only one is 'correct'.

Unit 15: Listening comprehension

Up the creek

Even today, when air and road travel has made Africa so readily accessible to Europeans and Americans, there are innumerable aspects of African life which tend to take one by surprise. The unfamiliar lurks everywhere, and the presence of Western culture seems merely to emphasise this unfamiliarity. Basically, the essence of our reaction to the strange, the unfamiliar, is a sense of fear. Every country contains landscapes that arouse unease – whether it be some remote Alpine valley, the wild lavender fields of Upper Provence, or a lonely Norwegian fjord at twilight. But in my own experience West Africa contains more weird and eerie regions – rain-forest, mangrove swamp, parched plains of red earth – than any other place that I have seen. It is not only in the foreigner that these landscapes evoke fear. A large part of all old African religions is devoted to placating the unknown and the unseen – evil spirits which live in a particular tree or a particular rock, a thousand varieties of ghosts and witches, the ever-present spirits of dead ancestors or relatives. I have myself been kept awake at night in Calabar by a friend from Lagos who was convinced that the witches of the east were out to get him, or that he was about to be kidnapped and eaten. During four and a half hours in a canoe along the creeks of the Niger delta, gliding over the still and colourless water beneath an equally still and colourless but burning sky, I, too, have experienced a sense of fear, or at least a sense of awe. Except for the ticking of the little outboard engine the silence was complete. On either hand stretched the silver-white swamps of mangrove, seeming, with their awkward exposed roots, to be standing knee-deep in the water. Where the creek narrowed you could peer deep into these thickets of mangroves – vistas secret, interminable and somehow meaningless. There was no sign of life except for the shrill screech of some unseen bird.

   I was on my way to the ancient slaving port of Bonny, which we reached in late afternoon. Scrambling up some derelict stone steps (slithery with slime and which had managed to detach themselves from the landing-stage so that you had to jump a two-foot gap to reach wet land), I found myself in an area of black mud and tumbled blocks of stone.

(From *The Sins of the Fathers* by James Pope-Hennessy)

Answers to 'Up the creek'

Multiple choice: 1b; 2c; 3d; 4b; 5c

True or false? 1. false; 2. false; 3. true; 4. false; 5. true; 6. false; 7. true; 8. false; 9. false; 10. false

Vocabulary in context: 1c; 2b; 3b; 4d

Expansion exercise

1. Air travel has made Africa available.
2. The unfamiliar lurks everywhere.
3. Our reaction to the strange is fear.

4. Every country contains landscapes that arouse unease.
5. West Africa contains more regions than any other place.

6. African religion is devoted to placating the unknown.
7. I have been kept awake.
8. I too have experienced a sense of fear.
9. The silence was complete.
10. You could peer deep into these thickets.
11. There were swamps of mangrove.
12. There was no sign of life.
13. I was on my way to Bonny.
14. I found myself in black mud.

Language building

1. Remind students of the phrase 'a sense of . . .', which occurs here several times: a sense of fear/awe.

2. Draw attention to the examples of words containing the prefix '-un', e.g.: *un*awares, *un*familiar, *un*familiarity, *un*ease, *un*known, *un*seen.

Likewise to the suffix '-less', e.g.: colour*less*, meaning*less*.
Elicit other words using this suffix, e.g.: senseless, harmless, tactless, homeless, defenceless, etc.

Both 'un-' and '-less' are easy to recognise and always have the same meaning:
 un- = not
 -less = without
They are therefore highly generalisable and can aid in comprehension.

3. a) *To peer* adds precision to the general verb 'to look at'. Ask these questions about 'peer':
Is it long or short?
Does it imply 'difficult to see'?
What shape are your eyes when you peer?

b) *To lurk* adds precision to the general verb 'to hide'.
Is it a nice or a nasty kind of hiding?
Is there something suspicious about lurking?
Does it also have some of the sense of 'wait for'?

4. *Landscapes that arouse unease . . .*
Ask students to listen for a phrase which is synonymous with this (. . . 'landscapes evoke fear'.)

5. *Swamp*
This word occurs in both Reading and Listening passages. In the Reading passage it is not possible to work out its meaning from the context, which tells us only that swamps are flat and low-lying. In the Listening passage, however, it is possible to deduce a number of further characteristics of a swamp:
it is wet
the water is still
it contains vegetation
it contains mud
This is a good example of the cumulative definition of a word through multiple contexts

6. *Creek* – can also be defined from context clues.

7. Draw attention to: 'slithery with slime'. 'Slithery' refers to a surface which causes someone or something to slip (e.g. the road was slithery). 'Slimy' refers to the *feel* of an object (e.g. the fish was slimy).

Discussion

1. Both passages were about places with a special 'atmosphere'. Have you ever experienced this kind of feeling?
2. Do you believe in the supernatural?

Unit 16: Listening comprehension

Answers to 'Population growth and industry'

Multiple choice: 1c; 2d; 3b; 4d; 5c

True or false? 1. false; 2. false; 3. true; 4. true; 5. false; 6. true; 7. false; 8. false; 9. false; 10. false

Vocabulary in context: 1: census; 2b; 3b; 4c

Open-ended questions

1. What is the main problem in compiling detailed world population statistics?
2. What was the population situation through most of human history?
3. Why did birth-rates suddenly overtake death-rates?
4. What characterises the population of industrial societies?
5. What might happen to population in the underdeveloped world if industrialisation does not take place?

Language building

1. Ask students to make a list of all the words and phrases to do with:
a) population
e.g. statistics, birth-rate, census, age-group, etc. . . .
b) economics/industry
e.g. technology, industrial, productivity, efficiency, etc. . . .

2. a) 'Rate' is commonly coupled with a number of other nouns apart from 'birth-' and 'death-', e.g.: divorce-rate, pulse-rate, infant mortality-rate, growth-rate, interest-rate, failure-rate, expansion-rate. This use of 'rate' can always be expressed in figures, e.g.;
'The failure-rate was 30 per cent'
'The death-rate was 6 per 1000'

b) Note: demo*graphy*, demo*grapher*, demo*graphic*. Construct similar series with: geography, photography, pornography, radiography.

3. Draw attention to the way many of the same words are either repeated, e.g. population, birth-rate, statistics,
or are re-expressed,
e.g. statistics/figures, slow down/drop/decline/reduce, population . . . increase/population explosion/population growth/growth of population/rise in population.
In a passage of this sort the *same* concepts are being called upon again and again, even

if they are expressed in slightly different ways. In other words, the passage is less difficult than it appears.

4. Note the highly *tentative* nature of many of the statements, e.g.:
... what they *think* happened ...
... they *believe* ...
... death-rate *may have been* due ...
... of what *may have been* universal ...
... the death-rate *could be* reduced ...
... it *seems almost* certain ...
... statistics *suggest* that the modern ...
... *If* the theory is applicable ... *we would* expect ...
... the death-rate *could* begin ...
... there *could be* a decline ...
... it is *just possible* ...
... *might be* influenced ...

5. The passage uses many phrases which generalise a reality, e.g.:
energy sources are primitive = people use wood and charcoal, which are not very efficient as fuel
decline in fertility = not too many babies are born

Get students to explain the full meaning of these condensed, generalised phrases:
– the phenomena of population
– advanced level of technology
– high potential growth
– a distinctive economic arrangement
– the population is stabilised

6. 'Biological laws *underlie* ...'
This sort of compound verb, from 'lie under', is quite common.
Draw attention to other examples: underpin, undermine, undergo, underwrite, undercut. In all of these verbs the prefix 'under-' refers to position: underneath, from below.
There are also common compound verbs formed with 'under-' where it means too little, not enough, e.g.: undercook, underpay, under-rate, underestimate, underfeed.
(See also the language notes to the Unit 15 Reading comprehension passage, 'The lost world of the Kalahari'.)

7. Infanti*cide*.
There is a small group of words which are formed with the suffix '-cide' (killing), e.g.: suicide, genocide, homicide, parricide, fratricide, matricide, regicide, pesticide.

Discussion

1. Do you agree with birth-control? Is it likely to be successful in underdeveloped countries?
2. Will underdeveloped countries be able to industrialise? What will happen if all countries become industrialised?
3. Why do people in underdeveloped countries tend to have large families?

The year 2000

It remains to be seen whether the reserves of raw materials would be sufficient to supply a world economy which would have grown by 500 per cent. South-East Asia alone would have an energy consumption five times greater than that of Western Europe in 1970. Incidentally, if the underdeveloped countries started using up petrol at the same rate as the industrialised areas, then world reserves would already be exhausted by 1985.

All this only goes to show just how important it is to set up a plan to conserve and divide up fairly natural resources on a world-wide scale.

This is a matter of life and death because world population is exploding at an incredible rate. By the middle of the next century population will expand *every year* by as much as it did in the first 1500 years after Christ. In the southern, poor, parts of the globe, the figures are enough to make your hair stand on end. Even supposing that steps are taken to stabilise world population in the next fifty years, the number of inhabitants per square kilometre will increase by from 4 in the United States to 140 in South-East Asia. What can we do about it?

In the first hypothesis we do nothing. By the year 2000, the southern parts of the world would then have a population greater than the total world population today. Calcutta would have 60 million inhabitants. It is unthinkable.

Alternatively, we could start acting right now to bring births under control within fifteen years so that population levels off. Even then the population in the southern areas would not stop growing for seventy-five years. And the population would level off at something like twice today's figure.

Finally, we could wait ten to twenty years before taking action. If we waited ten years the population of the southern areas would stabilise at 3000 million. Even today the number of potential *workers* increases by 350,000 people per week. By the end of the century this figure will reach 750,000. In other words it will be necessary to find work for 40 million more people per year – not to speak of food!

What this means in practical terms we can scarcely imagine. But clearly if we do nothing, nature will solve the problem for us. But at what cost!

Answers to 'The year 2000'

Multiple choice: 1b; 2c; 3b; 4d; 5c

True or false? 1. false; 2. false; 3. true; 4. true; 5. true; 6. true; 7. false; 8. false

Expansion exercise

1. The world economy would have grown.
2. Asia would have an energy consumption five times greater.
3. Reserves would be exhausted.
4. How important it is to set up a plan.
5. World population is exploding.
6. Population will expand every year.
7. The figures make your hair stand on end.
8. The number of inhabitants will increase by 4 in the States.
9. What can we do?
10. We do nothing.

11. The Southern parts of the world . . .
12. 60 million.
13. We could start acting now.
14. The population would not stop growing for twenty years.
15. The population would level off.
16. We could wait.
17. If we waited ten years . . .
18. If we waited twenty years . . .
19. Even today . . .
20. This figure will reach 750,000.
21. It will be necessary to find work for 40 million people.
22. We can scarcely imagine.
23. Nature will solve the problem.

Language building

1. Draw attention to the use of conditional forms throughout, including the use of conditional words other than 'if' (whether, even supposing, etc.)

2. Extract the following groups of synonyms relating to *population*:

to grow
to explode
to expand
to increase

to stabilise
to level off
to bring under control
to stop growing

Likewise the following words are all used to refer to *doing* something:
to set up a plan . . .
steps are taken . . .
do (nothing) . . .
start acting . . .
taking action . . .

3. There are a number of common phrases used which it is worth drawing attention to:
It remains to be seen . . .
this only goes to show . . .
in other words . . .
There are also two reasonably common idioms:
a matter of life and death
enough to make your hair stand on end

4. 'By' is frequently used throughout, in two different ways:
a) by a given quantity:
    by 500 per cent
    by as much as . . .
    by from 4 in . . . to 140 in . . .
    by 350,000 people per week

b) by a stated time in the future:
    by the year 2000
    by the middle of the next century
    by the end of the century

5. The tape should now be played again. Students should make notes. These should be used to rewrite a summary of the passage.

Unit 17:   Reading comprehension

Answers to 'Our first words'

Multiple choice: 1b; 2c; 3c; 4b; 5d

True or false? 1. true; 2. false; 3. false; 4. true; 5. true; 6. false; 7. false

Vocabulary in context: 1b; 2b; 3c; 4a; 5c

Language building

1. In this passage certain familiar words take on an extension of their customary meaning. The most striking examples are:

a) *critical* (critical period/times/stage) here has the meaning of vital, crucial, all-important.

b) *cue* is used here as a synonym for 'sign' or 'signal'.

c) *programmed* is more familiar as a noun; as a verb it means conditioned, adapted, or designed.

d) *dulls* is more familiar as an adjective; as a verb it means to deaden or devitalise.

e) *triggered* is more familiar as a noun; as a verb it means to set off, stimulate, activate.

f) *mothering* is normally a somewhat pejorative word, suggesting excessive care or spoiling; here it means, simply, maternal love.

2. Using nos. c), d), e) above, get students to practise making verbs from common nouns and adjectives. Remind them that adjectives are often turned into verbs by adding the prefix '-en', thus:

quiet – quieten	soft – soften
hard – harden	light – lighten

It should be pointed out that verbs derived from nouns (e.g. to trigger, to programme) are most common in technical and journalistic English. Examples of this are words such as:
to land (for aircraft, etc.)/beach/dock
to schedule/timetable
to shortlist/blacklist
to wire/pipe/string

3. Onomatopoeic words are often easy to learn, and, if used with discretion, bring unexpected life into one's speech. Draw students' attention to 'hubbub' (line 27), and 'babbling' (line 30).

Notice that in both words the 'bb' sound suggests confusion or lack of clarity. (A similar effect is achieved in Shakespeare's *Macbeth* at the opening of the witches' chorus: bubble, bubble, toil and trouble.)
Other onomatopoeic words connected with the sound of speech or laughter are:

chitter-chatter	giggling/sniggering
mumbling/murmuring	screeching/shrieking
howling/bawling/yelling	moaning and groaning

Discussion

1. What do you consider to be the main points of this article? Ask students to set them out in not more than three sentences.
2. The author speaks of 'critical times for acquiring skills'. What does he mean by this? Ask students to draw on personal experience in order to discuss the importance of these 'critical times' in learning one's mother tongue.

Unit 17:   Listening comprehension

Learning to speak

It is, everyone agrees, a colossal task that the child performs when he learns to speak, and the fact that he does so in so short a period of time challenges explanation.

Language learning begins with listening. Individual children vary greatly in the amount of listening they do before they start speaking, and late starters are often long listeners. Most children will 'obey' spoken instructions some time before they can speak, though the word obey is hardly accurate as a description of the eager and delighted cooperation usually shown by the child. Before they can speak, many children will also ask questions by gesture and by making questioning noises.

Any attempt to trace the development from the noises babies make to their first spoken words leads to considerable difficulties. It is agreed that they enjoy making noises, and that during the first few months one or two noises sort themselves out as particularly indicative of delight, distress, sociability, and so on. But since these cannot be said to show the baby's *intention* to communicate, they can hardly be regarded as early forms of language. It is agreed, too, that from about three months they play with sounds for enjoyment, and that by six months they are able to add new sounds to their repertoire. This self-imitation leads on to deliberate imitation of sounds made or words spoken to them by other people. The problem then arises as to the point at which one can say that these imitations can be considered as speech.

It is a problem we need not get our teeth into. The meaning of a word depends on what a particular person means by it in a particular situation; and it is clear that what a child means by a word will change as he gains more experience of the world. Thus the use, at say seven months, of 'mama' as a greeting for his mother cannot be dismissed as a meaningless sound simply because he also uses it at other times for his father, his dog, or anything else he likes.

Playful and apparently meaningless imitation of what other people say continues after the child has begun to speak for himself. I doubt, however, whether anything is gained when parents cash in on this ability in an attempt to teach new sounds. (From *Language and Learning* by James Brittan)

Answers to 'Learning to speak'

Multiple choice: 1c; 2a; 3b; 4d

True or false? 1. true; 2. false; 3. false; 4. true; 5. false; 6. true; 7. false

Vocabulary in context: 1b; 2a; 3b; 4b

Language building

1. Draw the attention of students to the fact that the speaker is watching his words. This is evident from the way in which he chooses his language. Point to the following phrases, which are all guarded expressions of approval or disapproval, or qualified assertions:
. . . everyone agrees . . .
. . . it is agreed . . .
. . . but since these *cannot be said* to show the baby's intention to communicate, they *can hardly be regarded* . . .
. . . it is clear that . . .
. . cannot be dismissed . . .
. . . I doubt, however, whether anything is gained . . .

These expressions all belong to the formal register of speech. Suggest less formal ways of saying the same thing, e.g.
. . . obviously . . .
. . . don't you think . . .
. . . surely/clearly/naturally
. . . don't forget (that) . . .
. . . I doubt . . .
Get students to look back at the Reading comprehension passage to find further examples of formal expressions of opinion.

2. Intonation and pronunciation
Play the tape through once again, asking students to listen carefully to the pronunciation of the following words:

explanation	indicative
cooperation	sociability

Remind them of the difference in stress between the above words and:

explain	indicate
cooperate	sociable

3. Note the use of the reflexive 'self-' in 'self-imitation'. Remind students of other common compounds using 'self-', e.g.:
self-confidence/assurance
self-conscious
self-sufficient
self-evident

self-service
self-government/management
self-opening/closing

4. Idioms and expressions
'. . . a problem we need not *get our teeth into*'
Check that students have properly understood this idiom (the meaning, here, is
'to grapple with' or 'analyse in detail'.)

Mention other common idioms associated with parts of the body, e.g.:
to put your back into
to put your foot into (it) . . .
to give/lend a hand
to have a finger in every pie
to escape by the skin of your teeth
to keep an eye on (somebody/something)

Expansion exercise

1. It is a task.
2. The fact challenges explanation.
3. Language learning . . .
4. Children vary greatly.
5. Late starters . . .
6. Most children 'obey' instructions.
7. Obey is hardly accurate . . .
8. Before they can speak . . .
9. Any attempt leads to difficulties.
10. It is agreed that . . . and that . . .
11. These cannot show the baby's
    intention . . .
12. They play with sounds.
13. . . . by six months . . .
14. This leads on to imitation.
15. The problem arises . . .
16. . . . we need not . . .
17. The meaning of a word depends . . .
18. . . . what a child means will
    change . . .
19. The use of 'mama' cannot be
    dismissed.
20. He uses it at other times.
21. Playful imitation continues.
22. I doubt whether anything is gained.

Discussion

1. Compare the Reading and Listening comprehension passages. On what points do
they agree? Are there any striking points of disagreement?
2. Consider the question of 'baby-talk', both in your own language and in English.
Are any words or sounds common to most babies?
Notice the striking use of *alliteration* and *repetition* in the baby-talk of English children,
e.g.:
choof-choof (train)   quack-quack (duck)
toot-toot (car)   puss-puss (cat)
Consider, also, the words invented by adults to make it easier for children to
understand, e.g. bye-byes (bed), kitty-cat, etc.

Unit 18: Reading comprehension

Answers to 'A sunrise on the veld'

Multiple choice: 1b; 2c; 3d; 4c; 5a

True or false? 1. false; 2. false; 3. false; 4. true; 5. true; 6. true; 7. true; 8. true; 9. false; 10. true

Vocabulary in context: 1a; 2b; 3b; 4c; 5c; 6b; 7a; 8c

Open-ended questions

1. Why did the boy think of the ants as being 'like glistening black water flowing through the grass'?
2. Why did he want to shoot the buck?
3. What made him decide not to shoot it?
4. What was the thought that made him angry and miserable?
5. Why did he say to himself: 'The ants must eat too!'?
6. Was he surprised that the ants finished off the buck so quickly?
7. Why did the boy 'fancy' that the ants turned and went away?
8. At the end of the passage the boy imagines the buck as it was early that morning. What brings this thought to his mind? Why did he think of the buck walking 'like kings and conquerors'?
9. What does he find difficult to believe?

Language building

1. This is a highly sensuous passage. Draw attention to the importance of colour, sound, feel and touch, and to the precision with which these sensations are conveyed. Notice, too, how often the same idea is reformulated or extended through different words, e.g.:

a) the ground was *black with ants*
. . . *like* glistening *black water*
. . . before he saw *the blackness* thin
big *black ugly insects*
. . . the *writhing blackness*

b) the writhing blackness that *jerked convulsively with the jerking nerves* . . .
. . . *small twitches* . . .
The buck could *no longer feel.*
. . . a *mechanical protest of the nerves.*

74

. . . the grass was whispering and *alive*
. . . great *energetic* ants . . .
. . . *hurried and scurried* towards the fighting shape.

Now, working from these sets of sentences, ask the students to *deduce* the meaning of:
writhing
jerk
twitch
hurried and scurried

2. *Hurried and scurried*
Repetition of this kind – usually alliterative – is not uncommon in English. Mention the following examples:
twisted and turned
moaned and groaned
fumbled and groped
(And the famous line from the tale of 'The Three Little Pigs':
'He *huffed and* he *puffed* and he blew the house down'.)

3. *Trickling*
Throughout the passage the ants are compared to water. Why? Where does the similarity lie?
If students do not understand the meaning of 'trickling' get them to study the following phrases in context:
. . . like glistening black *water flowing* through the grass
. . . ants *trickling back* with pink fragments in their mouths . . .
about the bones *the ants were ebbing* away

Prompt them with the following questions:
a) When the ants are hurrying and scurrying *towards* the fighting shape are they moving quickly or slowly?
b) And when they are trickling *back*?
c) When they are moving *towards* the buck do they seem to be a single body or a mass of scattered individuals?
d) And when they are ebbing *away*?
e) Which of the following could trickle?
   rainwater down one's collar
   a waterfall in spring
   a waterfall in a dry summer
   a burst waterpipe in the street
   blood from a wound
f) *Ebb* is connected with *tides*. When the tide is ebbing, is it coming in or going out?

4. One of the most remarkable features of this passage is the sense of time *present* which it gives us. Draw attention to the way in which nouns, verbs, and adjectives (almost instinctively!) take '-ing' endings. In some sentences there is deliberate repetition of '-ing' forms, e.g.:
. . . glisten*ing* black water flow*ing* through grass.
He could hear nothing but one bird sing*ing* and the . . . rustl*ing*, whisper*ing* ants.

. . . the writh*ing* blackness that jerked convulsively with the jerk*ing* nerves.
. . . a swell*ing* feel*ing* of rage . . .
. . . liv*ing* things dy*ing* in anguish . . .
bits of white . . . shin*ing* in the sun . . . glow*ing* over the rocks.

5. *He sternly controlled* . . . (line 21)
If students have difficulty with this sentence, ask them to say in their own words what the boy feels at this moment. Is he excited, disgusted, tired, curious?
Once they have grasped the idea that he is on the point of vomiting, ask them what it is that stops him from doing so? Is it his will-power?
What then is the meaning of 'sternly'? Is the word 'stern' associated in any way with the idea of 'authority'?

6. *Their pincers full of meat* (line 30)
Does it matter if you do not know the exact meaning of 'pincers'? It should be possible to deduce what 'pincers' are by asking:
a) Are they part of the ants' bodies?
b) If so, are they at the back or the front?
c) Are they an extension of the body (like legs and arms) or an integral part of it (like eyes and the mouth)?
d) In this text what do the ants use their pincers for?

Use a similar strategy to discover the meaning of 'frisking' (line 39) and 'sniffed' (line 39).

7. Notice how often 'the buck' is described obliquely, e.g.:
the fighting shape
the beast
the writhing blackness
the mass
the shape

And finally,
the skeleton
the bones

8. Point out the phrases in which the boy's thoughts are indirectly expressed:
It came into his mind that he *could shoot it* . . .
Why, the whole thing *could not have taken* longer . . .
It *might have been lying* there years . . .
. . . that was where the eyes *were* . . .
That morning . . . this small creature *had been stepping* proud and free through the bush . . .
Such a sure swiftfooted thing *could surely not be* trapped . . .?

9. Notice the deliberate mixture of styles, the colloquial directness of the boy's thoughts standing out against the richness of the description. Draw attention to useful phrases such as:
things like this happen . . .
I can't stop it.
There is nothing I can do.

Discussion

Trace through the passages the various changes of feeling the boy goes through. Try to decide in each case what gave rise to the feeling. Use the following phrases as orientation points:

a new fear (line 1)
he looked wildly about (line 2)
pity and terror seized him (line 5)
It was a swelling feeling of rage and misery and protest . . . (line 14)
He was glad . . . (line 18)
He sternly controlled the uselessly convulsing muscles . . . (line 21)
Why, the whole thing could not . . . (line 26)
He strode forward . . . (line 27)
'Go away', he said to the ants very coldly. (line 33)
. . . he thought incredulously . . . (line 36)
. . . feeling the chill on its skin even as he himself had done, exhilarated by it (line 38)
And then what had happened?

Unit 18:   Listening comprehension

Tiny killers on the march

The savagery of the soldier ant is a legend in Africa. I once saw a rat a foot long blunder into a column. In seconds it was wriggling in agony, covered in a thick black mantle of ants. Soon ants were moving back to their nest carrying tiny chunks of bloody flesh. Five hours later only the rat's bones remained. People groggy with sleeping sickness have been known to collapse near ants' nests: only skeletons are found next day.

Ants' nests line African rivers. On the surface of the ground, only a small indentation is visible, but below is a network of passageways that may extend as deep as ten feet. The Queen keeps court in the deepest and most secret recess of the labyrinth. More ferocious than any human king or queen, she reigns alone, after killing all other active females in the group. The males who come to fertilise her eggs are killed by her moments later.

Queens rarely make public appearances. They travel only at night, always escorted and even carried by the strongest and fastest ants.

The ants I was watching had occupied their nest for about three weeks, and were about to move. It was seven in the evening. The equatorial night descended abruptly, and the forest became still and quiet. Suddenly a nervous swarm of ants burst from the nest, and swiftly shaped themselves into a column about one and a half inches wide and moving at approximately ten feet a minute. The soldier ants formed the flanks; the workers were in the middle. Millions of ants had already passed when, within the column, a white stream took shape. This stream was made up of the tiny larvae – newly-born ants – being carried out of the nest by the workers. It was a sign that the ants felt secure. If I was lucky the Queen would soon follow.

Almost immediately I felt a surge of restlessness run through the column: a palace guard of soldier ants appeared, their antennae raised, their mandibles bared. Behind them, at last, came the Queen. She advanced slowly, dragging her huge belly, and swinging her head from side to side. I bent low to photograph her – so low that the enraged soldier ants were able to leap on to my camera. As I took four or five

exposures they swarmed over my face. I dropped my camera, and slapped madly at them. They died, but their task was done. When I looked at the column again, the Queen had disappeared into the black tropical night.
(From *The Observer* Magazine)

Answers to 'Tiny killers on the march'

Multiple choice: 1a; 2c; 3c; 4c

True or false? 1. false; 2. true; 3. false; 4. false; 5. true; 6. true; 7. true; 8. false; 9. true; 10. false; 11. false

Vocabulary in context: 1a; 2d; 3b; 4a; 5a; 6b; 7c; 8a

Language building

1. After letting students listen several times to the tape, draw their attention to certain similarities between the Reading and Listening comprehension passages, e.g.:

Reading	*Listening*
dying in anguish	wriggling in agony
pink fragments of flesh	tiny chunks of bloody flesh
only the rat's bones remained	it was clean-picked
a swarm of ants	a nervous swarm
their pincers full of meat	their . . . mandibles bared
. . . till he stood above the skeleton	only skeletons are found next day

2. Make use of the technique of *deduction* explained in the notes to the Reading comprehension passage to get students to work out the meaning in context of:
mantle
groggy
ferocious
chunks
mandibles/antennae

The following questions may be of help:

a) *mantle*
Can you see through a mantle?
Did the ants completely cover the rat?

b) *groggy*
If you have sleeping sickness how do you feel? Alert? Weary?
Is there any similarity between collapsing from drunkenness and collapsing from sleeping-sickness?

c) *ferocious*
What is the connection between this word and 'after killing all other active females in the group'?

d) *chunks*
Does this mean the same as 'fragments'?

e) *mandibles/antennae*
See notes on 'pincers' (Reading comprehension).

3. Some adjectives do not change their form when used as adverbs, e.g. 'I bent *low* . . .'
Other adjectives commonly used in this way are: hard, soft, long, loud, clear, clean, firm.

4. In this passage many nouns are used as verbs (and vice versa), e.g.: swarm, blunder, escort, shape, line, form, reign, surge.

This is a common feature of English, and students should be advised to learn how to derive verbs from nouns, or the reverse. Frequently there will be marked differences in pronunciation, even when the two words are written alike (e.g. 'escort'.) These should be mentioned. Occasionally, one form will have a wider range of meaning than the other (e.g. 'blunder', as a verb, means not only 'to make a mistake' but also, in a sense, 'to move clumsily', as in 'to blunder about'.)

Discussion

1. The soldier ant is described as being 'savage'. What other insects can you think of that might be described in this way?
2. Compare the Reading and Listening comprehension passages. What do they have in common?
3. Take five common insects and discuss them in terms of shape, colour, size, habits.

Unit 19: Reading comprehension

Answers to 'The secrets of sleep'

Multiple choice: 1b; 2c; 3d; 4b; 5d; 6b

True or false? 1. false; 2. true; 3. false; 4. false; 5. true; 6. false; 7. false; 8. false; 9. false; 10. false

Vocabulary in context: 1c; 2d; 3b; 4a; 5c; 6d; 7b; 8c

Open-ended questions

1. What effect has the invention of electricity had on sleep and sleeping habits?
2. Why is research into sleep difficult to carry out?
3. What is the function of an electroencephalogram?
4. What observable changes take place while we are sleeping?
5. Is there any proof that the patterns of sleep cannot be changed?
6. Why is jet-lag dangerous?

Language building

1. Ask students to find other ways of expressing the following phrases:
double his output
working round the clock
a familiar hazard
plays havoc with
a very hazy idea

2. Draw attention to the following phrases which are common, useful, and worth learning:
a good night's sleep
it's bad for you
that was about all you could do

3. When we 'mumble' we talk indistinctly, usually in a low voice. Words like this are often used with rhythmic effect, e.g.:
mumble and grumble
toss and turn
pick and choose

4. 'Insomnia' is the name of an illness. It is sometimes possible to work out the meanings of words formed in the same way from their roots, e.g.: anaemia, haemophilia, neuralgia, pneumonia, diphtheria, hysteria, etc.
Try to find other examples.

5. Notice the word 'overtired'. Remind students that many other words can be formed in the same way, that is, by the addition of 'over' or 'under', e.g.:

overfed	underprivileged
overpaid	undernourished
overworked	underdeveloped

Try to find other examples.

There was a joke in England at the time when many American GI's were in the country. It was said of them, 'They're overpaid, overfed, over-sexed, and over-here!'

6. Notice the rather formal sentence structures in these examples:

'Only when candles . . . *did* people seriously *start* . . .'

'Only in the last few years *have* experts *come up with*'

This reversal of the usual word order comes after phrases like 'only when', 'not only', 'so much', 'so fiercely', etc.

This formal structure, usually more common in the written language, is often replaced by this sort of sentence:

'*It was* only when . . . *that* people seriously started . . .'

7. 'Put people in *such* circumstances, and even though . . .'

What are the circumstances which 'such' refers back to? (See also the exercises on 'such' in the Reading comprehension section.)

8. Draw attention to the compounds:

output = production (i.e. that which is *put out* by work)

onset = start (i.e. that which is *set on* or set going)

The prefixes 'in-' and 'out-' plus a verbal element are frequently found as compounds in English, e.g.:

income	output/outlay
input	outflow
intake	outlet
inlet	outburst
inflow	outbreak
inset	outset

The prefix in all of these compounds has directional force. For example:

income = something which comes in (money)

outburst = something which bursts out (anger)

Discussion

1. Do you ever have vivid dreams? Try to describe one you have had recently.
2. Do you think there are any advantages in being an insomniac?

Unit 19:   Listening comprehension

Sensory deprivation in space

Experiments have been carried out on volunteers to see what happens when all sensations are stopped. This can be done in several ways. One method is to put a man inside a completely isolated room. This room is heavily sound-proofed and absolutely dark. There is no light or sound and the person is instructed just to lie motionless on a bed. People have stayed in rooms such as this for as long as four days. The results of sensory deprivation (SD) vary with the individual.

Soon after entering the confinement cell most subjects went to sleep and slept almost without interruption for ten to twenty-four hours. These are gross estimates for there was nothing by which the subjects could determine the time which had elapsed. We know for certain that one subject slept for nineteen hours but insisted that he had had a nap of less than one hour. According to the monitoring microphone, which was capable of picking up the deep breathing of sleep, it seems more likely that most subjects slept almost all of the first twenty-four hours.

We felt that so much sleeping in the first day wasted the effects of confinement, so we started placing subjects in SD early in the morning. We reasoned that after a night's sleep our confined subject would be unable to dissipate the effects of SD by sleeping. Such was not the case. As far as we could determine they went to sleep just as quickly and slept just as long as the previous subjects. We then started entering the subjects at midmorning, midday, and midafternoon. As it turned out, it made no difference when during the day and, presumably, during the night we started the confinement; the initial sleep period was always about the same.

We had not expected this extended period of initial sleep. In fact, it had seemed reasonable to expect something of the opposite. SD was a very novel situation for our subjects, and as such, we reasoned, it should have occupied them for some time. I had a similar expectation for astronauts during space flight and was greatly surprised to learn that the Russian astronaut Yuri Gagarin had been able to sleep during his space flight around the Earth.

Other effects were also noted. With no real sensations to work on, the brain makes up all sorts of false information. Many people experience vivid dreams and hallucinations. When they are finally taken out of the room into the real changing world of light and sound, they are in a very strange state of mind, ready to believe anything and not really able to make decisions.
(From *SpaceBiology* by C. F. Stoneman)

Answers to 'Sensory deprivation in space'

Multiple choice: 1c; 2d; 3a; 4a; 5c

True or false? 1. false; 2. false; 3. true; 4. false; 5. false; 6. true; 7. false; 8. false; 9. true; 10. true

Vocabulary in context: 1b; 2a; 3b; 4c; 5d

Language building

1. *Soundproof* means 'proof against sound', 'something which cannot be penetrated or affected by sound'.
Consider these words:

leak-proof	foolproof
burglar-proof	waterproof
child-proof	fire-proof
rust-proof	shock-proof

What do these words mean? Add a noun to each of them to show how they might be used, e.g. a *burglar-proof* lock.

2. *Nap* (also a verb, 'to nap') is a word which adds precision to the more general word 'sleep'.

Ask students to match the more precise words in column A with their more 'general' parents in column B.

A	B
jerk	bang
rap	throw
snap	push
snip	break
toss	cut
shove	pull

3. Ask students to listen for a phrase which means the same as 'a completely isolated room' (the confinement cell).

4. Draw attention to the fact that the phrase 'a completely isolated room' is clarified and expanded in the sentences which follow. Even if the word 'isolated' is not understood on first hearing, it is possible to work out its meaning from the context.

5. Ask students to listen for two examples of a verb which is used to mean 'we thought . . .' or 'we calculated . . .' (We *reasoned*)

Expansion exercise

1. Experiments have been carried out.
2. One method is to put a man in a room.
3. This room is dark.
4. There is no light.
5. People have stayed in rooms.
6. The results vary.
7. Most subjects went to sleep.
8. These are gross estimates.
9. One subject slept for nineteen hours.
10. Most subjects slept twenty-four hours.
11. We started placing subjects in SD early.
12. Our subjects would be unable to dissipate the effects.
13. They went to sleep just as quickly.
14. It made no difference.
15. We had not expected this.
16. It should have occupied them.
17. I was surprised to learn that Yuri Gagarin had been able to sleep.
18. The brain makes up false information
19. When they are taken into the real world they are ready to believe anything.

Discussion

1. Why were subjects put in a completely isolated room?
2. Why did the experimenters change over to putting subjects in SD early in the morning?
3. Why did the experimenters not expect subjects to sleep for so long?
4. What has this to do with space flight?
5. Why are subjects ready to believe anything when they leave the room?

Unit 20: Reading comprehension

Answers to 'The dangers of space'

Multiple choice: 1c; 2b; 3c; 4d; 5c

True or false? 1. true; 2. true; 3. false; 4. false; 5. false; 6. false; 7. true; 8. false; 9. false; 10. false

Vocabulary in context: 1a; 2c; 3b; 4b; 5c; 6d

Open-ended questions

1. Why is there less radiation on earth than in space?
2. Why is it so difficult to be sure about radiation damage?
3. What have solar flares to do with space travel?
4. Why were the Apollo crew worried about solar flares?
5. What is the long-term solution to radiation danger in space?

Language building

1. If necessary, students should be allowed to use their dictionaries to check the meaning of 'dose', 'spurt', and 'hazard'.
Ask them to suggest what nouns or verbs these words are most commonly associated with, and to combine these words in sentences.

2. 'Radiation is the greatest danger to explorers in space.'
'The atmosphere again acts as our protective blanket . . .'
Students should look for phrases which occur later in the passage as alternative expressions for the same ideas.

3. Do you know what a 'meteor' is? Can you guess? Does it matter whether you understand this word?

4. 'Makes our environment tolerable . . .'
The verb from 'tolerable' is 'tolerate'. Find a phrase in paragraph 2 which means the same as 'tolerate'.

5. Draw attention to the special scientific use of the words 'cell' and 'organ'.

6. *Accumulate*
Work on this from the context to answer these questions:
Does it involve acquiring or losing something?

Is it a sudden or a gradual process?
What kinds of things can be accumulated?

7. Deformed
Work on the meaning of this from the angle of word-formation clues:
form(ed) = shape(d)
      de- = taken away from, spoiled, etc.
Hence, deformed = spoiled shape

8. The tone of this passage is very cautious. Very few sentences express certainty.
Many express doubt or uncertainty, e.g.:
a very rough estimate
have reason to think
it is extremely difficult to be sure
we simply do not know
What other examples of 'cautious' language can be found in the passage?

9. Draw attention to the phrase 'the trouble is . . .' This is often followed by a clause
with (or without) 'that', e.g.:
'The trouble is (that) nobody knows the answer.'

Other phrases which behave in the same way are:
the problem is (that)
the difficulty is (that)
the intention is (that)
the implication is (that)
the suggestion is (that)

10. Notice the large number of *passive* constructions. Why do you think they are used
rather than active forms?

Discussion

1. Is there any future for men in space?
2. Is space exploration worth the money when we have so many problems on earth?

Unit 20: Listening comprehension

A near-disaster in space

Considering the enormous number of things which could turn a space mission into a
fatal disaster, it is remarkable that there have been so few accidents. 1967 was a bad
year; in January, the Americans lost three astronauts in a fire which occurred during
tests on the ground and, in April, the Russians lost astronaut Komarov landing after
sixteen successful Earth orbits. The accident was due to a parachute failure. Neither of
these tragedies was quite what the world had expected. It was feared that one day
astronauts would be stranded in space, alive but with no possibility of returning to
Earth. This very nearly happened in 1970 during the flight of Apollo 13.
    The life-support and other systems of spacecraft are interlinked. This means that if
one system fails it is likely to cause other systems to fail too. Designers have tried to

avoid disasters by duplicating, and in some cases triplicating, important pieces of equipment; for example, Apollo has no less than three fuel cells. Even so, a breakdown in the service module of Apollo 13 was nearly fatal. On 13 April one of the low-temperature oxygen tanks in the service module suddenly broke open; the explosion probably damaged the other oxygen tank close beside it. The exact reason for the explosion may never be known. The important point to note is that the oxygen from these tanks is not only used by the crew but also feeds the fuel cells, and the fuel cells produce electrical power and water. So, one failure immediately caused a major (but not total) power failure affecting nearly every system in the command module and produced a shortage of oxygen and water for life-support.

The safe return of the astronauts was due to their ingenuity and powers of improvisation. They managed to adapt their equipment. They were able to use it for different purposes from those for which it had been originally intended.

Intelligence and the ability to use limited resources for self-preservation have always been admired by writers of adventure books. The shipwrecked sailor who converts bits of wreckage into a raft and an explorer who makes a bow and arrow from branches and bootlaces are considered heroes because they survive by their own wits. Many people thought that the advanced technology of space flight ruled out all opportunities for makeshift repairs, but Apollo 13 proved them wrong. Luckily, at the time of the accident the lunar module was still joined to the command and service modules, and the lunar module had most of the things urgently needed by the disabled modules. The spacecraft was not on a free return trajectory, one which would bring it round the moon back to Earth, and rocket power was needed to bring it into such a trajectory. Without a proper power supply, the rocket of the service module could not be fired; the rocket of the lunar module had to be used instead. Inside this module there was a supply of oxygen, water and power, and a guidance system. Though it was designed for a crew of two for only about thirty hours, and intended for landing on the moon, this vehicle became the lifeboat of Apollo 13.

Life for the three crew members was difficult but bearable. A lunar module cannot re-enter the Earth's atmosphere without burning up, so the crew had to return to the command module, jettison their lifeboat and the service module, and turn themselves into the right position for re-entry, hoping that their heat-shield had not been damaged by the explosion of the oxygen tank. Re-entry and recovery were totally successful.

(From *Space Biology* by C. F. Stoneman)

Answers to 'A near-disaster in space'

Multiple choice: 1c; 2b; 3d; 4c; 5b

True or false? 1. false; 2. false; 3. true; 4. false; 5. false; 6. true; 7. true; 8. false; 9. false; 10. false; 11. false

Vocabulary in context: 1b; 2b; 3c; 4d; 5c; 6b; 7a; 8b; 9a and c; 10b; 11a; 12b; 13d

Language building

1. *Interlinked*
Collect examples of other uses of the element 'inter', e.g.:
inter-school (sports)
inter-university

inter–county
inter–disciplinary

2. *Parachute failure/power failure*
Both these phrases appear in the extract. 'Failure' frequently occurs with other nouns too, e.g.: heart failure, engine failure, crop failure, etc.

Attention should also be drawn to the simile of failure, 'breakdown', which is also used in the extract.

3. '*No less than* three fuel cells'
Another way of saying this would have been: '*As many as* three . . .'

4. *Breakdown* = the fact of breaking down
There are other words formed on the same principle, e.g.: a breakthrough, a breakup, a break–in, a break–out.

Which of the above could be applied to these phrases?
. . . of the famous pop–group
. . . at the Bank of England
. . . in cancer research
. . . at Dartmoor prison

5. '*The important point to note is that* . . .'
This is a very common way of introducing what is to come. Similar introductory phrases whose function is to tell the listener that something important is coming are:
'The problem is that . . .'
'The trouble is that . . .'
'What we have decided is that . . .'
'What I want to know is . . .'

6. Draw attention to the technical language used in the passage. This can be divided into two kinds:
a) truly technical words, only used in their technical sense, e.g.:
command module
spacecraft
trajectory
b) words which are often met with in general contexts but which are given a special technical meaning here, e.g.:
cells
fail
heat shield
tank

7. Draw attention to the way in which one sentence, or phrase, is often followed by another one which expands or describes it in more detail, e.g.:
'1967 was a bad year . . .' (followed by examples of what happened that year)
'It was feared that one day astronauts would be stranded in space . . .' (there follows an appositional clause expanding on the meaning of 'stranded')
'Designers have tried to avoid disasters . . . triplicating important pieces of equipment; for example . . .'

'The safe return of the astronauts . . . powers of improvisation.' (The whole of the next sentence is a rephrasing of this idea.)

'Intelligence and the ability . . . of adventure books.' (The whole of the next sentence gives concrete examples of this.)

'The spacecraft was not on a free return trajectory . . .' (In case we do not understand this, it is rephrased in the next clause.)

Expansion exercise

1. There have been few accidents.
2. 1967 was a bad year.
3. It was feared that . . .
4. This nearly happened in 1970.
5. The systems are inter-linked.
6. This means . . .
7. Designers have tried to avoid disasters.
8. A breakdown was nearly fatal.
9. An oxygen tank broke open.
10. The oxygen is not only used by the crew. . . .
11. One failure caused a power failure.
12. The return of the astronauts was due to ingenuity.
13. Intelligence has always been admired.
14. Space flight rules out repairs.
15. The lunar module was joined to the service module.
16. The spacecraft was not on a free return trajectory.
17. The rocket could not be fired.
18. It was designed for two.
19. Life was difficult.
20. A module cannot re-enter the atmosphere.